His Pride, Our Fall

His Pride, Our Fall

RECOVERING FROM THE TRUDEAU REVOLUTION

Kenneth McDonald

KEY PORTER BOOKS

The publisher gratefully acknowledges the assistance of the Canada Council, the Ontario Publishing Centre, and the Ontario Arts Council.

Canadian Cataloguing in Publication Data

McDonald, Kenneth, 1914–

    His pride, our fall : recovering from the Trudeau revolution

ISBN 1-55013-714-X

1. Trudeau, Pierre Elliott, 1919–   . 2. Canada – Politics and government – 1968–1979.* 3. Canada – Politics and government – 1980–1984.* I. Title.

FC625.M34 1995   971.064'6   C95-931631-0
F1034.2.M34 1995

Key Porter Books Limited
70 The Esplanade
Toronto, Ontario
Canada M5E 1R2

Typesetting: Heidy Lawrance Associates
Printed and bound in Canada

95 96 97 98 99 6 5 4 3 2 1

My experience of politics – that it impinges on individuals in three phases – is, I suspect, typical. Phase One is between the ages of seventeen and twenty-two, when idealism reaches its peak and the evils of the world are as plain to see as are the grand solutions. Phase Two extends from twenty-three, and serious entry to the workforce, to the late forties or early fifties during which marriage, career, and family relegate politics to a background associated with taxes and earning power. Phase Three starts when the children have left home and there is time for reflection. What was it all about and who has been doing what to whom?

In my Phase Three, what has been done to Canada by a corporal's guard of proud men from Quebec has been front and centre since Pierre Trudeau erupted on the national stage thirty years ago. That his dominant influence upon events has been tragic for Canada is an accident of history that this great country will recover from in time. But the fact that he was able to do those things shows how even the most apparently durable institutions can be undermined.

If Canadians are beginning to understand what has been done to them in the name of a national unity which served only to disunite, it is due to handfuls of patriots who put their Phase Three to good use.

This book is dedicated to them.

Kenneth McDonald

Of all our passions and appetites, the love of power is of the most imperious and unsociable nature, since the pride of one man requires the submission of the multitude.

— EDWARD GIBBON

· ONE ·

When Great Britain permitted its new French-speaking Canadian citizens to keep their language and forms of local government, it established a tradition that has endured: Canada is above all a place where people tolerate their neighbours and settle differences by peaceful means.

This is not to say that the differences are trivial or transitory, merely that even the lasting ones take on the character of familiar players, sometimes centre stage, sometimes in the wings, but always in the cast and always confining their combats to the written or spoken word.

A bequeathed tradition has been shaped into a Canadian characteristic by successions of immigrants who treasured the chance to partake of it. Yet the source, and the evolving framework of the common law that underpins it, are now hidden behind a wall of duality that conceals its Canadianness.

When Church gave way to State as the dominant power in Quebec, the Canadian federation was faced with a continuing paradox: a Quebec government which instinctively practices centralization of political power within its own sphere must always resist any move by the national government toward a centralization of power that would embrace Quebec. This was the paradox that led to the wall's erection. A circumstance that called for statesmanship was sidled up to in a manner reminiscent not of Charlottetown in 1867 but of Munich in 1938. A federal commission was mandated "to recommend what steps should be taken to develop the Canadian Confederation on the basis of an equal partnership between the two founding races...." [1]

That elaborate fiction was soon translated into "two founding languages" and the resulting legislation – picked at and reinforced by successive national governments without once consulting the people on the specific issue – has so irritated the Canadian majority that by 1992 a commissioner (Mr. Spicer) was astonished to report,

"The extent of consensus against official language policy is remarkable. [Official bilingualism] is rejected almost universally."[2]

The fiction was followed in short order by an event without parallel in a parliamentary democracy: the basis upon which that democracy was founded was changed 180 degrees by a device, transparent in retrospect, that enabled the government of the day to impose its will upon the people. Canadians who until then had enjoyed the individual freedom within the law that had been intrinsic to their British heritage since before Magna Carta – the Great Charter of 1215 – were suddenly restricted to certain government-defined "rights and freedoms" that would be subject to interpretation, and therefore further limitation, by government-appointed judges.

University of British Columbia professor Alan Cairns wrote that since the Charter was imposed "both federalism and parliamentary government [had] lost relative status in the constitutional order" through what he called a "profound wrenching transformation."[3] It was composed of two elements. First was the document's spurious title, the Canadian Charter of Rights and Freedoms, a cynical misuse of words that was calculated to persuade Canadians – and has succeeded in persuading perhaps a majority of them – that they didn't have any rights or freedoms until the Charter was granted them by a benevolent government. Second was the bestowal of government-guaranteed "rights" that enabled members of identifiable groups to demand redress through the courts if they thought they were being discriminated against, or if they thought their condition should be "ameliorated," all at the public expense.

Why was this done? On October 12, 1978, in the Commons debate on the throne speech, Prime Minister Trudeau said, "It is vital to me that it (the constitution) does give protection to the kind of linguistic equality that this government has put into the statutes (the Official Languages Act)." In the Commons on October 30, 1978, the Hon. James Richardson quoted that passage and then said, "What does the Prime Minister mean by 'give protection'? Clearly, he means that he wants to give protection from parliament. He wants to protect his legislation from any amendment by a future parliament. He wants to place his legislation beyond the reach of parliament....I receive thousands of letters from Canadians on this subject, and the people of Canada do not want the supremacy of a Trudeau-written constitution to replace the supremacy of a democratically-elected parliament."

In April 1992, on the tenth anniversary of the Charter's signing, *Le Devoir*'s editor Lise Bissonnette disclosed that "[former prime minister Pierre] Trudeau's entourage admits today that these [linguistic] clauses were the primary reason for the entire exercise."[4] Her disclosure reconfirmed Mr. Trudeau's triumphant declaration in a speech on the Constitution in December 1981: "We've got all the aces. We've got the right of disallowance, declaratory power, expropriatory power under peace, order and good government. And we've got the entrenchment of both official languages, which can never be removed. We've got French in the educational system of every province."[5]

"We" in that statement is also open to interpretation. It could mean "We, the Government of Canada." It could mean "We, the ten first ministers (Quebec's being absent) who cobbled the thing together." It could mean "We, the Liberal Party insiders who plotted and schemed to whip the Canada Bill through the British House of Commons to give our device a semblance of legitimacy." Given the imperial attributes of the speaker, it could mean "We" in the royal sense. What it could not mean, even though the speaker himself had made an off-the-cuff remark about the idea of a referendum on the topic, was "We, a majority of the Canadian people." Nor could it mean "We, representing governments that were elected with a mandate to change the Constitution," because none of the ten had such a mandate and the eleventh, Quebec Premier René Lévesque, who did have one, was left out of the accord by a trick.

From the fiction of two founding races, through the linguistic malarkey that flowed from it, to the 180 degree change in governance that was designed to perpetuate it, to a gradual realization that the whole business was contrived to authenticate the fiction – in a single generation we have been subjected to radical change.

What went wrong? How did we, a people cradled in individual freedom under the law, allow ourselves to be hornswoggled into a political condition not merely of servility but of a feudal servility in which two-fifths of our income is sequestered by governments that spend more than half of the gross domestic product?

How it happened is the subject of this book. Here it is enough to say that the rot started in the mid-1960s when former prime minister Lester Pearson imposed a British-style national health scheme on the provinces by threatening to withhold the proffered 50 percent federal share of costs if they refused. This unleashed two powerful forces. First, provincial governments, no longer restricted by the British North America Act's section 92 to borrowing on their sole credit, were suddenly able to spend money they had no need to raise through taxes. And second, the citizens who used the growing range of unpriced social services were persuaded they were "free." Those two forces combined to form a third: an alliance of consumers and politicians determined to maintain "a seamless web" of social programmes neither would admit a responsibility to pay for.

Today we live in a nominally federal system that was centralized to a point where the Constitution's division of powers no longer serves. As author Colin Campbell wrote: "The creation of [new ministries], all between 1975 and 1979, marks perhaps the most furtive expansion of central agencies the world has yet experienced."[6] Provinces were seduced into yielding important powers — and responsibilities — to a national government that borrowed on the public credit of Canada for purposes not of investment but of consumption. A national debt of staggering proportions has been accumulated from borrowings that were literally eaten away. The official inflation index is touted to be at record lows while the real inflation index is propelled by ever rising taxes to pay ever growing interest bills on national and provincial governments' debts.

If we stand back for a moment and survey the past thirty years, we see a series of little men hacking away at a monument — the British North America Act — that served the Dominion well for its first century. Jealous of Canadians' inheritance of British history, indeed of Canada's history, they sought to efface it and substitute their own concocted symbols as if Canada were but one more instant state of the United Nations. Dominion Day became Canada Day and the BNA Act itself became The Constitution Act.

Unlike those little men, the Canadian framers of the BNA Act understood that matters closest to people's hearts are best left close to the people for decision. National matters are properly exclusive to the national government, but affairs of the heart — home and property, safe streets, doctors and hospitals, schools, worship, and language — are properly exclusive to provinces and municipalities.

The very fact of local control establishes the principle of competition that fortifies a federal system. Freedom brings improvement and innovation not only in the private sector but in the public as well, yet how often do we hear yearnings for "a strong central government"? When former Alberta premier Ernest Manning charged that after imposing a national health scheme the Pearson government "would bring in grocery care next," the question was implicit: who in his right mind (outside the since defunct Soviet Union and the Liberal Party of Canada) would impose a national food distribution scheme against which it was illegal to compete?

At the outset we admitted that our differences are neither trivial nor transitory. Nowhere was this more evident than in the results of the 1992 referendum on the Charlottetown Accord. Far and away the highest "Yes" vote (73.6 percent) was in Prince Edward Island which depends on the national government for most of its revenues. The highest "No" vote (67.8 percent) was in British Columbia which is one of the three net contributors to equalization payments. Trying to equalize outcomes breeds discord between regions just as it does between individuals. The referendum itself was a travesty of referendum practice in, for example, Switzerland and the United States, where the people vote on specific issues. In Canada we were asked to vote "Yes" or "No" to a document aimed at rewriting and adding to a constitution that had already been transformed by the Charter's imposition. Small wonder Pierre Trudeau was vehement against tampering with his handiwork. But we the majority voted "No" for many reasons, and surely not least against the prospect of perpetuating yet more government at the beck and call of yet more special interests and their so-called entitlements.

The Charlottetown Accord exemplified what is wrong. It would have further complicated and rigidified what should be plain and flexible. By contrast, the BNA Act describes the distribution of powers, accords the French language due place, requires intra-Canadian free trade, and provides for the creation of new provinces. In short it is flexible enough to accommodate not only the aspirations of a Quebec that has dominated federal politics in the past, but also the aspirations of Western provinces that will outweigh Quebec's influence in the future.

The British North America Act stands as a monument to all that is good in the Canadian tradition. The shortest road to recovery from the Trudeau Revolution is to scrap his fraudulent Charter and restore the BNA Act to pre-eminence in Canadian affairs. Pre-eminence, not supremacy, for the fulcrum upon which that 180 degree turn was contrived was the alien concept of a written Constitution, as near unamendable as makes no difference, that was imposed as "the supreme law" upon a nominally self-governing people without either their prior consent or subsequent approval.

It is often said that because the BNA Act is clearly a document, it is also a written constitution. On the contrary, the Act is about what the different levels of a federal system of government are to be responsible for. It is not about freedom of the individual, or freedom of speech, or freedom to move and carry on one's business, because it is defined from the outset as expressing the desire of "the provinces of Canada, Nova Scotia and New Brunswick...to be federally united into One Dominion under the Crown of the United Kingdom of Great Britain and Ireland, with a Constitution similar in Principle to that of the United Kingdom."

The United Kingdom's Constitution is not a separate written document. It consists of the body of law — the common law — that has accumulated over the centuries from particular decisions arrived at from the particular opinions of juries and judges in particular cases that were brought before the courts. All of these, in their turn, established precedents that guided later decisions by later juries and judges. But enveloping and guiding the whole was the law-making body of Parliament, which could make or unmake any law whatever. Thus is the Constitution of the United Kingdom a creature of the people's elected representatives who make the laws, and who can change them to fit the changing circumstances of the times. It is not, as Mr. Trudeau asserted of his Charter, a document for "entrenchment" of specific statutes such as language laws "which can never be removed." On the contrary again, the things that are entrenched are the principles of responsible government which are the fruit of British history and which ensure that law-making is in the hands of the living as well as the dead.

France, by contrast, favours written constitutions (in a speech in 1977, Mr. Trudeau said defensively that it had "seventeen of them in 170 years") which define what the citizens are allowed to do in accordance with certain "rights" the state bestows on them.

The difference between the two was described by the French diplomat and author Alain Peyrefitte in his book *The Trouble with France*: "In Britain, Holland, Switzerland and the United States, guarantees of individual rights are as inexpugnably binding as a private contract. They are supported by the force of tradition. They were not wrested from the state, but the state is their guarantor. In our French hierarchical system, rights are either unilaterally bestowed and thus revocable, or else they are wrested violently from the state or the privileged and so threatened by counter-violence."[7]

In Canada's centennial year, the Canada Year Book described the BNA Act's origin: "Characteristically British is the lack of specific 'bill of rights' clauses in the Act and of any legal definition of the principles of responsible government — such fundamental features of parliamentary government being considered deeply entrenched in British common law, in the customs and usage, and in convention already operative in the federating provinces."[8]

It is true that the BNA Act is similar in some respects to the Constitution of the United States. Both describe the distribution of powers; both prescribe a federal state. The differences derive from their historical origins. Americans were concerned to limit the powers of all governments. Canadians recognized parliamentary sovereignty but having witnessed the secession-fed strife south of the border, they recognized also the need for the dominion government to be supreme. Hence the vesting of its power "to make Laws for the Peace, Order, and good Government of Canada" in relation to all matters not assigned exclusively to the provinces. This led the English jurist, A. V. Dicey to observe that "...undoubtedly the powers bestowed on the Dominion Government and Parliament are greater when compared with the powers reserved to the Provinces than are the powers which the Constitution of the United States gives to the federal government. In nothing is this more noticeable than in the authority given to the Dominion Government to disallow Provincial Acts." Nevertheless (and as Dicey also remarked) when dominion and provincial parliaments failed to agree on particular aspects of their respective powers they looked to the law for resolution and "the Courts inevitably [became] the interpreters of the Constitution."[9]

But unlike the United States, which devised and applied its own amending formula, Canadian governments were unable to agree on one. Resolutions had to be sought from the United Kingdom's Judicial Committee of the Privy Council. Thus when in 1931 The Statute of Westminster recognized the independence of self-governing countries of the Commonwealth, Canada asked to be excepted and continued in its curious role of an independent country obliged to turn elsewhere for approval of any proposed change to its constitution. This, as we shall see, was later advanced as the justification for the events of 1981–82, when closure was used in the Canadian Parliament to propel the Canada Bill toward eventual passage by the British Parliament. This, in turn, entrenched in the Canadian constitution an amending formula to which the government of Quebec had not agreed.

That Mr. Trudeau should have gone to such lengths to change the country's basic law is entirely consistent with two traits of his public character. One – consistency – was expressed by his friend Jean-Pierre Goyer: "I know Trudeau best by what he's written – and it's the best way to know him. He doesn't deviate from his writings. Just about everything he thinks is there."[10] As he wrote in his *Memoirs*, "On the whole, the Constitution Act largely enshrined the values I had been advocating since I wrote my first article in *Cité libre* in 1950."[11]

The other trait — arrogance — was brought out by author Colin Campbell in his description of events leading to "patriation" when Trudeau's advisor Michael Kirby called it "a once-in-a-life-time opportunity to effect comprehensive constitutional change (and perhaps unblock the process), and, as such, should not be lost."[12] Campbell commented that the claim of a once-in-a-life-time opportunity took on meaning "only when we consider that Trudeau had attained the age of sixty-one, after twelve years of sporadically attempting patriation and reform. Urgency directly stemming from Trudeau's desire to retire from politics with honour brought about the federal move."[13]

Which brings us to federalism and what it is thought to mean in the minds of different people.

In his book *The Tyranny of Words*, Stuart Chase wrote: "The point of every discussion is to *find the referent*. When it is found, emotional factors dissolve in mutual understanding. The partici-pants are then starting from a similar foundation, talking about similar things."[14]

If one fact stands out from the ritual slanging matches over Quebec's and Canada's futures it is the absence of a referent among the participants.

Much is made of differences between secession, separation, sovereignty, and sovereignty association as regards the aspirations of Quebecers, allegedly almost half the total, who wish to sever relations with Canada, or at least some relations, or if not now perhaps later.

But nothing is made of the difference between the majority, however slim, of Quebecers who don't want to do those things, and who call themselves federalists, and other Canadians who wish to keep the country together and who call themselves federalists as well.

The difference is in the assumed role of the national government; whether it is to be The Grand Redistributor of tax revenues and borrowed money, or merely the arbiter of national affairs that are inappropriate to the provinces.

In our search for a referent we might turn to Felix Morley's seminal work *Freedom and Federalism*, in which he wrote: "The essence of federalism is reservation of control over local affairs to the localities themselves, the argument for which becomes stronger if the federation embraces a large area, with strong climatic or cultural differences among the various states therein."[15]

Morley's definition fits nicely with sections 92 and 93 of the British North America Act, which gave the provinces exclusive powers over local affairs. Section 91 accorded the national government authority over all matters not reserved to the provinces, and then enumerated those national matters. (See the Appendix for the Act's provisions.)

This division of powers was breached in the 1960s and 1970s by the national government's imposition upon the provinces of "universal" social programmes which infringed provincial authority and were subsidized first with federal revenues and soon afterwards with money borrowed on the public credit of Canada: the prime source of our present debt.

Between 1964 and 1975 the federal civil service grew 65 percent, from 200,000 to 330,000, and established the base for the furtive expansion of central agencies that author Colin Campbell remarked upon.[16]

The architects of that expansion could be called many things, but federalists they were not.

Is Prime Minister Jean Chrétien, who was prominent among those architects, a federalist today? He says so; he may even wish to make concessions to Quebec that would be consistent with the functioning of a federal state, but hanging over him all the time is his record from the 1980 referendum on sovereignty.

In the House of Commons Debates of April 17, 18, and 21, 1980, he spelled out the material benefits showered upon Quebec from the national coffers. For example: "Quebec will receive in 1980 more than 50 percent of the whole equalization program...; the energy policy of this government has saved the province of Quebec no less than $6 billion since 1974...; Quebec pays at most 22 percent of the federal taxes; Ottawa pays 55 percent of the Quebec health budget; Quebec received 35 percent of the funds allotted to public welfare schemes in Canada; 75 percent of the family allowance cheque to Quebec mothers comes from the federal government...; Quebec gets more family allowances and tax credits than it pays out in taxes."

Fourteen years later, when a Quebec provincial election was called and pro- and anti-sovereignty forces were drawn up at the hustings, the federal cupboard was bare, and Mr. Chrétien made a point of not wanting to talk about Quebec. But quietly, and courtesy of a $6 billion make-work "national infrastructure" programme of which $2.8 billion had been awarded by the time of the election call, he had managed to slip one-half of the $2.8 billion into his native province.[17]

Thus to Jean Chrétien, as it has meant to his predecessors and let us hope not many of his successors, federalism means a strong central government that not only busies itself with affairs that are supposed to be exclusive to the provinces, but busies itself particularly with the affairs of the province that is particularly jealous of its exclusiveness.

This leads us to the matter of Quebec's significance in the political equation, how its bloc vote dominates federal politics, and all the ramifications of that inescapable fact. Therefore, it is only proper for me to declare my personal view of the relationship between French-speaking Quebecers *as individuals* and other Canadians. I believe the test is a simple one, one that many of us must have experienced, yet one that to my knowledge has been and to this day is still missing from the voluminous literature.

To apply it, set yourself in a foreign country among foreigners, let us say in an airport departure lounge or at a bus terminal. All around, and at intervals through the public address system, is the sound of foreign tongues. The passing throng is composed of Europeans, or Russians, or Africans, even of Americans or Australians or New Zealanders. Beside you, you discover, is a traveller from Chicoutimi, or Quebec City, a traveller you hail with joyous cries that are at once re-echoed, for you both have lighted upon a fellow Canadian. You may struggle with French, he or she with English, but the visions that flow past your minds' eyes have this in common: they are of Canada. It is the land that unites you.

Preying upon domestic extensions of this joyous scene is the politically inspired myth of duality. We who live in Canada are self-evidently Canadians. We may choose to live in Quebec or Saskatchewan, but it is our choice and we are as free to move to or from those places as our ambitions and talents incline us. Or rather, we were as free. For when the revolution began it was ordained that Canadians were no longer one but two peoples who were divided by language. This manufactured division would be bridged by requiring public servants in all the manifestations of expanding government to become proficient in the languages of both peoples. The country and its government were to be "irreversibly bilingual."

Since "perfect bilingualism is an ideal that is sometimes approached but almost never attained,"[18] this decree introduced barriers not only to movement but to personal advancement as well. For it soon became apparent that if Canadians whose mother tongue was English were to apply for the increasing government, or government-related, positions that were designated "bilingual," it would not be enough that they were as "bilingual" in French as their French-speaking confrères were "bilingual" in English. To get the job, they would have to be francophones, that is, people whose mother tongue was French. In short, as we shall discover, the everyday matter of language, which people everywhere accustom themselves to in their individual circumstances, and in which they become as proficient as those circumstances demand if they are to earn a livelihood, was forced on an open society as a requirement for government service not to make the society more open, but to close parts of it off.

Since the closed-off parts tended in the nature of things to house the higher ranks of the civil and military services, a steady shift into those ranks of native French-speakers was inevitable. By 1989, the Public Service Commission's Annual Report showed francophone representation in key departments of the federal government ranging from a low of 19.7 percent in Defence through 48.3 percent in the Privy Council Office and 62.4 percent in the Public Service Commission to a high of 72 percent in the Office of the Official Languages Commissioner, while in 1994 the defence minister huffed that no one would pass beyond the rank of lieutenant-colonel unless he or she were fluently bilingual. Nor was this discrimination limited to the federal government. A year later a member of the Civil Liberties Association in Pontiac, Quebec, reported that "Our local Hydro Quebec unit hasn't hired an English-speaking citizen for over 16 years. This is an area of over 90 per cent English-speaking residents, many of whom may boast of from five to ten generations on their soil. Overall, the Quebec government employs less than one per cent English, while the composition norm previously was closer to ten per cent."[19]

Lest readers interpret this as a rant against the French language, or worse, against French-speaking Canadians, I should declare my bias: it is for freedom of the individual to do or say anything that is not forbidden by the law; and against the use of arbitrary power to prevent that freedom's exercise.

John Stuart Mill has a nice phrase that would sit well on the desk of Canadian prime ministers: "The liberty of the individual must be thus far limited; he must not make himself a nuisance to other people."[20]

In his sixteen years of office Pierre Elliott Trudeau made himself a nuisance by inserting the tentacles of government where they had no place to be: in the private lives of the citizens. The man who declared that there was no place for the state in the bedrooms of the nation set about making its presence felt in every room of the house. When he took office, after a century that included two world wars, the federal budget was in balance and the national debt was about $20 billion. By the time he resigned rather than face the electorate, and after sixteen years of peace during which spending on defence had declined from about 20 percent to 10 percent of the total, the deficit was 54 percent of revenues and the debt had increased tenfold to $200 billion. By 1991, and despite successor governments' modest efforts to control spending, an average prime rate of 10.46 percent had compounded Mr. Trudeau's debt into $400 billion.[21]

But that was only the fiscal result of the Canadian Revolution. How the whole business was set in train is examined in the next chapter.

· TWO ·

Apologists for the welfare state attribute its encroachment upon Canadian traditions to a spirit of the time that infected all Western industrialized nations in the 1960s. It is as good an excuse as any, and it is true that among Western intelligentsia Sweden, which led the way into the business, was upheld as the example to follow. Anyone who had a passing acquaintance with the upper levels of Ottawa's expanding bureaucracy could hardly escape the general air of veneration for what the Swedes were doing.

By coincidence, I knew something of Sweden from having been assigned the job, some fifteen years before, of comparing its air force with that of Britain's Royal Air Force, after *The Daily Telegraph*'s defence correspondent had alleged that the latter used six times as much manpower per aircraft as the former. In fact, the roles of the two were quite different: the Royal Swedish Air Force was concerned with home defence of its historic neutrality; the RAF with overseas and maritime commitments as well as home defence, and strike forces for offensive operations. Despite the differences in role, I found that if the RAF were to do the same job as the RSAF, but to the RAF's manning scales, it would have used 19 percent more people, not six times as many. Most of the difference lay in the staff: the RAF established many more people in headquarters formations than the Swedes did, and the reason for it was cultural/historical.

Culturally, the Swedes, with about eight million people running a modern industrialized society, were instinctively cost conscious. Neutrality imposed on them, as it does on the Swiss, a large degree of self-sufficiency, especially in armaments for defence, and if they were to achieve some sort of balance they had to be competitive enough in price and quality to sell the stuff abroad. So that was one thing: they couldn't afford to waste resources, whether material or human, and they went to great lengths to husband them. Then again, they hadn't been at war for almost 150 years, so that none of their three services had experienced the wartime expansions and subsequent contractions that tended to leave war-inflated staffs in place afterwards. For example an RSAF Group Headquarters, with one night and five day fighter stations under command, each housing three squadrons, consisted of seven officers and two airmen/civilians. For the same task, an RAF group HQ would have employed eighteen officers and 106 airmen/civilians. The RSAF group did its job by personal supervision, by delegating considerable responsibility to station commanders (who were given money and manpower budgets within which to hire and fire people and run the station) and by keeping paper work to a minimum. One group commander said that he had no wish for his HQ to become a post office, and that he wrote very few letters to his stations. On inquiry, I found that "very few" was less than ten a year; he did his job by flying to the stations – in all weathers in a front-line aircraft – and seeing for himself.

In the three weeks I spent among those fine fellows I got a lasting impression of people devoted to hard work, to economy of effort in order to achieve the utmost from limited resources, and to independence. How then, could they fall for the illusion that the great French economist Frédéric Bastiat expressed so well? ("The state is the great fiction by which everybody tries to live at the expense of everybody else.") The short answer is that those in Sweden who commanded opinion were converted by the socialist prophets, notably Gunnar Myrdal and his wife Alva, whose influence, as well as the results, are made painfully clear in William Gairdner's best seller *The Trouble With Canada*.[1]

The longer answer is one that applies also to Canada, and it is found in attitudes that are natural enough among the young, but much harder to explain among the middle-aged.

To an observer of mankind, who sees that some people are poor while others are rich, it may seem obvious that the rich should share some of their wealth, and if they are reluctant, surely a just society should require them to do it. From this seemingly natural inclination has sprung the idea that is central to the political Left and to the doctrine called socialism.

In the July 1, 1979, issue of *Freemen Digest*, Editor Michael Lloyd Chadwick wrote an article, "The Age of Democratic Socialism", in which he described the nature and history of socialism and its different forms. Thus communism was socialism pursued by revolutionary means, democratic socialism was socialism pursued by peaceful or constitutional means, and national socialism was socialist dictatorship with the emphasis on nationalism rather than internationalism. "In Germany nationalism was called Nazism, which was socialism pursued in a rigid political environment, similar to fascism." In a discussion of the strategy of democratic socialism, Chadwick quoted E.F.M. Durbin, a noted socialist, who asked: "If the economic system is in urgent need of reform, and if the maintenance of democracy is an essential condition of social justice, how can the one be used to secure the other?"[2]

The answer was by using the power of the State, but to do it gradually, by democratic means, that is, by persuading growing numbers of people to vote for policies that promised them material benefits.

Socialism attracts because it appears to combine charity with justice. Thus charitable reporters or commentators who learn from the state's statisticians that when the total of Canadian families is divided into five quintiles, the highest get ten times as much income as the lowest, and that the top two quintiles together get two-thirds of all income, they are likely to conclude that something should be done to even things out.

If they also subscribed to the individual Canadian's inherent right to freedom under the law and to the enjoyment of property, they would admit that whatever was done must be done voluntarily. But then they would not be socialists.

Even though statisticians have also come to our aid by showing that forced redistribution of wealth and incomes doesn't work, that in fact it adds to the rich group without doing much for the poor – but doing a lot for the growth of the state – it is still illusory because it ignores what happens to the individuals of which the groups are composed. Some move up, some down; every living soul is different and unique and intrinsically defiant of statisticians. (As Jonathan Swift wrote in a letter to Alexander Pope, September 29, 1725, "I hate and detest that animal called man; although I heartily love John, Peter, Thomas, and so forth.")

At the root of socialist theory is the conceit that clever men and women can so manage the affairs of a nation as not only to overcome the ups and downs of the business cycle but also to smooth out the different material outcomes that stem from everyone's different abilities and talents. It is just a matter of using the power of the state to enforce a redistribution of wealth and income between individuals and regions.

This conceit, which infected Canada's policy-makers in the mid-1960s and had its first expression in "universal" medicare, was to culminate fifteen years later in the "equalization" provisions of Mr. Trudeau's Charter of Rights and Freedoms. They invoke the power of the state in "promoting equal opportunities for the well-being of Canadians; furthering economic development to reduce disparity in opportunities; and providing essential public services of reasonable quality to all Canadians." They also commit the State "to the principle of making equalization payments to ensure that provincial governments have sufficient revenues to provide reasonably comparable levels of public services at reasonably comparable levels of taxation."

Consider for a moment how those lofty phrases are to be brought to life. The state is personified by politicians who make the laws and civil servants who are charged with administering them. Is it not apparent that when citizens in one part of the country discover that their well-being suffers by comparison with that of citizens in another part, they would be justified in complaining to their Member of Parliament; that he or she would be justified in seeking whatever remedies were available from the catalogue of "equalization" or "regional disparity" programmes; and that civil servants would then be required to draw resources from those programmes so as to equalize opportunities for the well-being of the citizens who complained? Is it not apparent that when elected officials of one township discover that the state has used public funds to "further economic development" in another township, they will call upon their Member of Parliament to do likewise for them? That when these marvels have nudged their way into public services which were already being pressed to become comparable with others previously extended, that the public service will expand everywhere? And that when a multitude of these events has occurred, and public services have been dreamed up and put in place from east to west and north, the resulting game of leapfrog will have evolved into one of beggar-my-neighbour?

Nowhere in this fantasy-land of a state-invoked panacea for mankind's imperfections did the clever men who cobbled together "The Supreme Law of Canada" mention a political economy's two essential ingredients: property and the creation of wealth. In that omission, in the bland assumption that the wherewithal to effect all the redistributions is a given, that the redistributions and ensuing state interventions will not affect it, and that people will continue to go about their businesses with undiminished energy regardless of the taxes the state is siphoning from their incomes – in that omission is gathered the fallacy of the theory.

A free market economy is one in which a freely elected government is responsible for the underpinnings that enable its people to create wealth. Among them (commonly called infrastructure) are the following: a legal system that protects everyone's property rights and under which everyone is equal; maintenance of a stable currency; schools and hospitals to which everyone has access; installation of roads, airfields, harbours, and navigation facilities; and other means of communication that serve the whole society.

Within that economy the people are free to earn incomes from trade and exchange; and from those incomes, which the government's infrastructure enables them to earn, they contribute the taxes to pay for it.

Property and the creation of wealth; the first is misunderstood, the second neglected. Property, to the socialist, is things: houses, estates, automobiles, airplanes – objects no doubt of envy to those who lack them, or have fewer of them, or have some of inferior size or quality. Those things are an expression of wealth, which in turn has accumulated from income, which abounds within the top two quintiles that get two-thirds of all Canadian income and are made up of rich people from whose (higher) taxes the redistributions can be effected; that is to say, the proportion of income that is taxed must rise with the income.

This is regarded as "fair taxation" and "equitable" when it is manifestly unfair and discriminatory. The purpose of taxation is to pay for the government infrastructure that enables people to create wealth. Everyone benefits from it in proportions that vary from person to person and household to household, but it is safe to say that the proportions of benefit will closely resemble the differing incomes: the higher the income, the greater the use of highways and airports, or of consulates and embassies abroad, of law courts, even of garbage collection. For that greater use, those with higher incomes should pay more than those with lower incomes, and if the amount needed to pay for the services is 20 percent of all the incomes added together above a certain minimum, all should pay their 20 percent. The $30,000 earner would pay $6,000; the $60,000 earner $12,000; the $150,000 earner $30,000 and so on.

But that would be at odds with the doctrine that "ability-to-pay" be interpreted as "ability-to-pay-more-if-you're-richer-than-I-am," a cardinal point in the politics of envy that socialism embraces.

Inevitably, rich people are identified with the business enterprises, large, medium, and small, which create the nation's wealth, and this brings us to that six-letter word from the socialist lexicon: profit.

To the Left, it is represented by a cartoon in which a fat man wearing a tail coat, striped pants, and top hat, his waistcoat strained by the weight of a gold watch chain, is carrying a bag marked PROFIT as he sneaks from the back door of the factory in which his employees are working their impoverished bodies another step nearer the grave. What he does with the profit is implicit in the cartoon: he keeps it for himself.

This, no doubt, created the justification for the tax on the profits of a corporation, the word corporation being a natural candidate for abhorrence by its association with fatness in general and in particular with boardrooms where fat men in tail coats disport themselves at the workers' expense.

Canada's economy has suffered great damage at the hands of administrators who misunderstood, some of them for political reasons, this matter of profit. How much it should be taxed, the fact that when none is declared a corporation has no profits tax to pay, the temptation to increase costs (for example by borrowing) in order to reduce or eliminate the tax, arguments as to whether a corporation is a "fiction" that cannot be taxed and merely passes it on to consumers, the ability of corporations to defer taxes which then grow into interest-free government loans – all these distortions of a free market economy stem from prejudice against property and the creation of wealth and from the consequent desire to redistribute those essential ingredients of a political economy.

The truth is that three elements – business enterprises, wage/salary earners, and investors – combine to create wealth. Each of them earns income, and each of them owes the same proportion of income to the government in return for the services that have contributed to their production and consumption activities. [3]

Now Lester Pearson, who was at Canada's helm when the rot started, was a diplomat, by all accounts a nice fellow, great sense of humour, and so on. But a diplomat, whose calling requires him to be nice most of the time and firm occasionally, is firm on those occasions at the instance of his political masters at home. It is not his finger that wags, but his government's. Even as minister of external affairs in the St. Laurent government, although he was the acknowledged expert, his official words were those of the cabinet. When he became prime minister, his principal interest was "in international affairs and in the ideas of his 'civilized' friends, who ranged all over the ideological map." [4] One of the ideas came from his policy advisor, Tom Kent, who wanted to introduce a national health service similar to that of his native Britain. But what could be done by Britain's unitary government manifestly could not be done by the government of a federal state in which the provinces held exclusive powers under Section 92 (7) of the BNA Act for "The Establishment, Maintenance, and Management of Hospitals, Asylums, Charities, and Eleemosynary Institutions in and for the Province, other than Marine Hospitals."

That wise provision supplied the element of competition I mentioned before as fortifying a federal system. Improvement and innovation flowed from the passage of ideas. Moreover, the fact of provinces' borrowing powers being limited to what they could get on their own credit imposed a healthy fiscal prudence upon their governments. The instinctive urge of politicians to bribe voters with their own or borrowed money was constrained by the market's assessment of provinces' creditworthiness, that is, on the market's assessment of their ability to repay money they borrowed against the future soundness of the provincial economy. In short, although a political economy can never be as confined by balance sheets as a private business, it must in general be guided by the principle that guides all businesses, namely economy of effort.

Economy of effort, besides being one of the principles of war, is also one of Nature's laws. As Warren Blackman once remarked, "throughout all the natural laws which govern natural phenomena there exists one over-riding principle and that is that Nature always directs her affairs with an economy of effort, and it is precisely this economy of effort, which means the attainment of the highest possible level of efficiency, that the businessman shares with Nature in his attempts to remain solvent."[5]

Kent was rescued from the BNA Act's constitutional bonds by fellow mandarin A.W. (Al) Johnson, who explained that all he had to do was to define the principles of a national health scheme to which provinces would then be required to adhere if they wanted to get the 50 percent of costs that would be held out to them. If they didn't adhere to the principles, they wouldn't get the money.

This quiet little administrative device, which needed no constitutional amendment to bring it into effect, was just the thing to persuade a prime minister beset with a raft of domestic problems and an election to fight. As Kent wrote afterwards, "It was so simple in concept but so effective."[6]

It was also the crack in the dyke of Canadian fiscal responsibility, with only Finance Minister Mitchell Sharp making brave but fruitless attempts to postpone the flood, and Ontario's Premier John Robarts fearing that the quality of health care might be prejudiced by the "stampede" into medicare for the federal government's electoral advantage. (Kent noted that the provinces generally were more concerned about their prospective shares of the Health Resources Fund than the medicare plan itself.) The political advantages were plain. Provincial governments whose health insurance schemes had been self-financing were now relieved of the political responsibility for raising half of the costs for schemes they would naturally seek ways of extending for their own electoral advantages. The federal government was led to believe that costs could be contained by making periodic assessments of provincial per capita costs, striking an average, and docking payments to provinces that exceeded the average. Apparently no one considered the rather obvious corollary that as costs rose with the advance of medical science, as costs rose with the stimulus of proffered medical services that were both universal and "free," and as costs rose with the stimulus of vote-catching at election times, the "average" would rise too until the only means of containment would be a combination of cutbacks and rationing. Moreover, the fortifying element of competition was eliminated: alone among the industrialized nations, the provision of basic private health care was made illegal in Canada. Meanwhile, the increases in the federal government's "share" of costs that were constitutionally outside its proper responsibilities would strain its revenue-raising capacity to the point where it would have to borrow on "the public credit of Canada." In other words, provincial governments were shown a way to spend borrowed money without having to borrow it themselves against their own credit.

Borrowing money for investment purposes is a fact of everyday life. It is borrowed, let us say, for the extension of a manufacturing plant, or for the purchase of new or improved machinery. The new plant capacity, or the new machinery's contribution to efficiency, increase the entity's productivity, and from its growing income it pays back the loan. The borrowing has made it possible for the entity to create new wealth. This is a basic difference between borrowing in the private sector and the public. While it is true that when governments borrow money for certain public purposes they contribute to the creation of wealth, they do so indirectly by increasing the productivity of the private sector. A municipal government borrows money to build a road and lay sewers so that private contractors can build houses or industrial plants in which taxpayers live and work. From the wealth those taxpayers create they pay taxes from which the municipality repays the money it borrowed. Also, when governments borrow money for supporting services such as education and health, the resulting increases in, or maintenance of, productivity among the populace contribute indirectly again to the creation of wealth and thereby to the taxpayers' ability to pay the government's bills.

But whereas in the private sector creditworthiness, and eventually the ability to stay in business, depend upon the tangible factors of sales and markets, assets and liabilities, the factors affecting the public sector are intangible.

A provincial government borrows money to meet current expenses and repays the loan from taxes, but until recently it refrained from borrowing more than it judged could be recaptured from taxes because to do so would affect its credit rating: if the rating fell, it would have to pay a higher rate of interest on future loans, and its operating expenses would rise. But when Canada's national government borrows it does so against the public credit of Canada in its entirety, against the capacity of the whole of the Dominion and its people to generate enough wealth to keep up the interest payments. If foreign lenders begin to doubt that capacity, they will reduce or stop their lending. But unless the government-as-borrower cuts its borrowing requirement by cutting its spending, it will have to compensate by borrowing more at home and still keep adding to its interest costs.

This, incidentally, illustrates the fallacy of forced redistribution. In theory, money is redistributed from richer to poorer. But when you rob Peter to pay Paul, Peter is discouraged from working harder while Paul doesn't need to work as hard as he did before, or even at all. The economy begins to contract, tax revenues decline, governments borrow to make up the difference by selling bonds to the private banks, and guess who buys the bonds from the banks? Not Paul, who is a recipient of some of the borrowed money, but Peter who has been discouraged from taking the risks that are inseparable from the creation of wealth and is looking for a safe return on his dwindling capital. And as the borrowing grows, and the interest bill grows with it, so does the government's presence grow as well, leading to the comment of the French economist Bertrand de Jouvenel: "The more one considers the matter, the clearer it becomes that redistribution is in effect far less a redistribution of free income from the richer to the poorer, as we imagined, than a redistribution of power from the individual to the State."[7]

This was the course Canada embarked on under the captaincy of Lester Pearson. When Al Johnson and Tom Kent showed him how to subvert the constitution in principle while appearing to uphold it in practice, they cleared the way for his successor to change it fundamentally. How easy it was to persuade the many that their wants could be supplied at the hands of a few, that when nobody had to pay at the counter for what the state provided, all its provisions would be free, and that all they had to do was to keep voting for the politicians who had not only promised those wonders but seemed to be delivering them.

Canadians whose forebears had wrested civilization from the wilderness, and whose sole requirement of government was that it be good and keep the peace, were persuaded that it could do far more than that; they had only to ask. Once they were taught to ask (and as the material rewards for doing so mounted), their changing concept of government changed them as well. Bit by bit, a hardy and independent people began to shift responsibility for themselves and their families into a growing dependence upon the state. Belief in their own abilities and strengths gave way to a realization that this new partner proffered not only security, but security for life.

That the proffered security was purchased with borrowed money raised no objection from those who had become used to asking for more. Citizens who would no more think of robbing their neighbours than of breaking their windows had long accepted the proposition that some neighbours could be rewarded at other neighbours' expense provided the rewarding was done at second or third hand by the impersonal agencies of the state.

There was nothing new in this. Fifty years ago, when Friedrich Hayek wrote his classic study of socialism, The Road to Serfdom (it was dedicated "To the Socialists of all Parties"), he had witnessed the effects of its culmination in Fascist Italy and National Socialist Germany. But when, ten years later, he wrote a foreword to a new edition, he had behind him six years of socialist government in England, which "have not produced anything resembling a totalitarian state." Then he continued, "But those who argue that this has disproved the thesis of The Road to Serfdom have really missed one of its main points: that the most important change which extensive government control produces is a psychological change, an alteration in the character of the people. This is necessarily a

slow affair, a process which extends not over a few years but perhaps over one or two generations."[8]

This is what I have seen happening to Canadians under the
influence of proud men who thought they had all the answers.
For thirty years, their allies have been a left-leaning media and
Canadians' inherent attributes of politeness and tolerance.

In the summer of 1993, when the Canadian Labour Congress,
the Action Canada Network, and other activists of the political Left
mounted a mass demonstration in Ottawa, the journalists of
Ontario's leading newspapers were urged by their union leaders
to join it. This bias to the left merely confirmed the findings in an
unpublished survey by Peter Snow of the University of Western
Ontario's Graduate School of Journalism in 1982 of 118 print and
electronic journalists in Ottawa's Parliamentary Press Gallery. The
largest group – 37 percent – felt closest to the New Democratic
[socialist] Party, 17 percent were Liberals and 11 percent Conservatives. But 43 percent saw themselves as in the political centre
and 42 percent as left of centre; only 4 percent as right of centre. Eighty-five percent thought that in some cases government
ownership was more desirable than private ownership. Asked if
there was too much government ownership of the economy, 64
percent disagreed. Asked if there should be laws for closer control of labour unions, 55 percent disagreed. Two-thirds favoured
laws for closer control of corporations.[9]

Not that bias in the media is a conspiracy. Journalists who
learn their trade from tenured professors will absorb the product
not of minds bent to the creation of wealth but of minds bent
toward its distribution. A university, after all, is a forum for ideas.
Although some of the faculties are concerned with wealth-creat-
ing functions such as engineering or agriculture or business, those
are rarely the choice of aspiring reporters or commentators; their
spawning grounds are the social sciences and the humanities, all
good things, but all concerned with the generality of people, with
mankind in the abstract.

Even though the collapse of collectivist regimes in Eastern
Europe and of welfare states in New Zealand and Sweden has
punched holes in the socialist balloon, Canada's home-grown
socialists are determined to patch it. It may have collapsed in

those countries, but that was because they didn't follow the instructions.

The truth is that those countries did follow the instructions, and that was why it collapsed. It harnessed the arbitrary power of the state to force people to do things they didn't want to do, plundered the enterprising to subsidize the lazy, and diverted unsustainable portions of the national wealth to the state and its agencies.

Once started, the growth of the state is not easily reversed, and this brings us back to the media.

For some years I have kept a file called Culture and Advertising. At first sight, the two topics might appear to be distinct. In fact, they are closely linked by the power of the state. Consistently over the past many years Canadian governments have been the country's largest source of advertising. Print and electronic media depend upon advertising for revenue. They also keep an arm's length relationship with commercial advertisers; that is, so long as ads meet certain standards of propriety and reasonable accuracy, they'll be printed or aired, and the advertisers are indifferent to the publishers' editorial opinions.

But when the state advertises, that's another story. Not only is it the largest customer, it also sets the rules that affect the publishers in a myriad ways: tax policy, regulations of every kind, subsidies and grants, customs and excise, trade.

This doesn't necessarily mean that editorial comment will support or oppose the state's policies. What publishers *will* do all the time, day in and day out, is publish what the State's spokespersons say and do and write.

A study by John Miller, Chairman of Ryerson University's School of Journalism, in 1990 revealed that "'official' news or institutional news made up 93.2 percent of the content of the *Toronto Sun*, 84.5 percent of the *Toronto Star*, and 80.2 percent of *The Globe and Mail*."[10]

Now feed in the fact that the state's share of Canada's economy has risen from about 20 percent in 1960 to about 50 percent in the 1990s, a growth of 150 per cent[11], and we see how successful the approach to socialism has been in the hands of Liberal and Progressive Conservative governments stealing the clothes of the NDP — and getting it faithfully reported by the press. Certainly the media apply their own biases. But they merely reinforce the leftward bias that comes from reporting the doings and sayings of politicians who speak with one voice for a continual growth of the state.

It is a paradox of reporting in Canada that the leftward bias is so encompassing that most of the media is unaware of it. In my file are examples upon examples where reporters describe people or activities as right-wing, or ultra-right-wing, or neo-conservative, or even neo-Nazi, but never as left-wing, or ultra-left-wing, or neo-communist. To be of the left is so much the norm as to be equated with the centre.

Yet I believe that most Canadians, given half a chance, would reject the opinions and political stances of extremists from left *or* right. That extremists of the left are not regarded as extreme, while extremists of the right are stigmatized, merely emphasizes how dangerous it is to label anyone. Because the left is never labelled it becomes the norm; the centre is on the left.

To take a recent example, when George Bain's book *GOTCHA!*[12] was published in November 1994 I faxed a review of it to Cheryl Cohen, Books Editor of the *Globe* on November 9, and backed it up with a mailed copy and the conventional stamped addressed return envelope. In the review, I mentioned the author's reference to authoritative studies which showed that three-quarters of big-city journalists between the ages of twenty-two and forty-five described their political ideology as "moderate left," and only one-eighth considered themselves "conservatives." The book also examined the *Globe*'s coverage of specific news "events," such as the Tainted Tuna Scandal, the Sinclair Stevens affair, and the Getty series, to show how easy it had become for editors and reporters to move from dubious allegations through confident assertions to accepted facts while omitting the elementary process of back-checking the allegations that started the stories off.

Since I enjoyed the book, and since its main theme (the subtitle is *How The Media Distort The News*) confirmed my own experience, I concluded that "George Bain has done Canadian journalism a service that puts publishers, editors, and reporters in his debt. Let us hope that many of them will read and mark his book.

Readers who are not journalists will appreciate his warnings."

I didn't hear from Cheryl Cohen, but on December 17, 1994 the *Globe* published a review of the book by David Hayes, who had written a book called *Power and Influence: The Globe and Mail and the News Revolution*. After admitting that, "Not surprisingly for someone of Bain's stature, many of his observations ring true" and that "Bain's detailed reconstruction (of the *Globe*'s Getty series) makes a convincing case for how the reporters – and, in its editorials, their paper – made too much of very little, at Getty's expense," Hayes continued, "But Bain's writing has a dyspeptic, bitter tone, like a father lecturing his son on the superiority of the good old days." He went on to assert that none of the studies about journalists' political persuasions had "satisfactorily proven that this affects their professional judgements," cited a former press critic for *The Los Angeles Times* in support, chastised Bain for being "irrational on the subject," thought that some of his "arguments are wonky," accused him of "woolly interpretations," and after quoting Bain's remark that "the CBC and *The Globe and Mail* hang together like a pair of testicles, the seminal influences, as they like to think of it, in national political journalism," Hayes concluded that "some of Bain's notions [were] a lot of cock and bull."

Hayes's review, and the *Globe* editor's omission from it of the book's subtitle, which might at least have predisposed readers toward the book itself, made a pretty good job of confirming Bain's theme. Two days after Hayes's review was published I faxed a letter to the *Globe* in support of the book, with quotes from my own experience. The letter was not published, nor did the *Globe* publish any letter on the topic of a book which had so much to say about the *Globe* that the paper's name topped the mentions in the index (twenty-nine times), just ahead of the CBC (twenty-six times). In Bain's chapter on *The Valour and the Horror*, he wrote "*The Globe and Mail*, in an inspired demonstration of editorial hypocrisy, said, 'Certainly the merits of *The Valour and the Horror* have been debated at length in the newspapers.' That was enough to make a plaster statue gag..."

To his credit, the *Globe*'s national affairs columnist Jeffrey Simpson, in a year-end review of political books, gave Bain's book the pride of place it deserved. Although he "respectfully dissented" from Bain's view that the media contributed in a major way to defeating the Conservatives, he threaded many of Bain's thoughts through his long article and took issue on his own account with Stevie Cameron's best-selling attack on the two Mulroney governments, *On The Take*. [13] He called it "patently uneven. There is no weighing of evidence, nor any attempt to provide context, balance or even understanding." In short, Simpson reinforced Bain's complaint with his own observation of the Cameron book. To illustrate the lack of balance, Simpson disposed of Cameron's thesis that the Mulroney Conservatives had "done something quite new in Canadian politics, whereas a quick glance at the Trudeau Liberals in Quebec would reveal a record of patronage, pork-barrelling and favouritism that helped continue the pre-Mulroney Liberal quasi-hegemony in Canadian politics."

Despite the media's slant to the left, it is self-evident that the political centre must be somewhere between liberals' desire for peaceful reform and conservatives' inclination towards precedent and order, and if both support individual freedom under limited government, it follows that any to the left or right of them must be moving towards an extreme.

In Italy before 1922 and in Germany before 1933, communists and Fascists or Nazis competed for the same type of mind. Benito Mussolini has been described as "a reluctant fascist because, underneath, he remained a Marxist." Friedrich Hayek quotes Adolf Hitler as declaring in a public speech as late as February 1941 that "basically National Socialism and Marxism are the same." [14]

Whether the means are revolutionary or gradual, ideologues of the Left seek similar ends. Canada's political elites have shifted the locus of state action from a modest 20 percent to a commanding 51 percent in one generation. [15] For those of us who lived through that shift it might have seemed gradual, but set against a preceding century of democratic capitalism under limited government it is clearly revolutionary. Not revolution by the governed, but revolution from the top down, using the appearances of democracy to bring about radical change.

Let us examine the way it was done and who the revolutionaries were.

· THREE ·

The job was done in four stages.

In Stage One, Lester Pearson surrendered to the St. Lawrence Seaway workers' demand that their wages be raised by 35 percent in one year to give them equality with their American counterparts. His personal mediator awarded them 30 percent, soon afterwards the postal workers threatened to strike if they didn't get 39 percent before Christmas, Pearson gave federal civil servants the right to strike, and a leap-frogging process by public and private sector unions destroyed the wage gap that had compensated for Canada's inherently lower productivity vis-à-vis the United States.

In Stage Two, Lester Pearson was persuaded by Tom Kent and Al Johnson to subvert the Constitution by establishing health care standards that provinces must comply with if they were to get the 50 percent of costs of a universal health scheme that Ottawa held out to them. This lured provincial governments into spending programmes they couldn't afford but were happy to fund with money that Ottawa first paid for from taxes and later borrowed for them on the public credit of Canada.

In Stage Three, Lester Pearson set up the Bilingualism and Biculturalism Commission to appease malcontents in Quebec, and failed to meet Quebec Premier Daniel Johnson's challenge, as Professor David Bercuson noted, "with a declaration that the Canadian federation was indivisible."[1] Then he changed the immigration rules to discriminate in favour of applicants from the Third World. Both things were done without consulting the electorate.

Stage Four saw the elevation of Pierre Trudeau to what Pearson called the near-dictatorial office of prime minister. ("When he has an assured majority in the House of Commons, the Canadian prime minister is the nearest thing to a dictator – if he wants to be one."[2])

With very few exceptions, Canada's print and electronic journalists portrayed as a run-of-the-mill Liberal the man whose commitment to socialism had been spelled out in his book of essays published the year he took power. Nowhere is his professed contempt for the journalists whose attention he coveted and secured, nowhere is it more roundly justified than in their failure to detect and publicize the consuming political philosophy of Pierre Elliott Trudeau. In one man was epitomized Felix Morley's definition of the contradiction between federalism and socialism: "Socialism and federalism are necessarily political opposites, because the former demands that centralized concentration of power which the latter by definition denies."[3]

Yet this consummate political strategist was able to use federalism for his centralizing purposes precisely as he foretold the method to a slumbering media.

In his book he maintained that radicalism could more easily be introduced in a federal state than in a unitary one[4]; in fact that federalism enabled "socialist governments" to be planted "in certain provinces, from which the seed of radicalism can slowly spread." Slowly was the watchword, because it would be foolish to try to "swing the whole country at the same time and in the same way into the path of socialism...."[5]

Taxation was no longer a means of recompensing government for the services it provided to help the citizens create the wealth upon which the whole society depended. Instead it was to become the equalizing agency in the hands of the state as Grand Redistributor. "A concept of [federal/provincial] tax sharing that does not take into account the beneficiary's needs...makes a mockery of the equalizing function of taxation and identifies itself as completely reactionary."[6]

He regarded as outmoded the historic socialist call for "Collective control and ownership of the vital means of production and seeking to achieve through state action the coordinated control of the economic forces of society."[7] In his view, there were "more flexible processes of economic control and redistribution."[8]

The man who found electioneering "a bit of a bore"[9] used his strategic genius to mold the process to his purposes. "... so long as socialism is to seek fulfilment through parliamentary democracy, with its paraphernalia of parties and elections, there will be a constant need for the tactician as well as the theorist. And both will have to be reconciled by the strategist."[10]

Portrayed by the media as a run-of-the-mill Liberal, Trudeau used his office to centralize political power in Ottawa, to impose official bilingualism, and to change our system of government. This, the imposition by fraudulent means of an alien form of government through a virtually unamendable written constitution, was the process that clamped us into the collectivized welfare state which bedevils us today. Had it not been done, had the BNA Act not been subordinated to Trudeau's written Charter, a combination of the BNA Act's division of powers, of the evolutionary common law, and of Parliament's power to make or unmake any law whatever would have permitted repeal or reform of Pearson's – and many of Trudeau's – follies to suit changing circumstances.

Trudeau knew that his Official Languages Act of 1969 was merely statute law that could be amended or repealed by a later sovereign Parliament. Therefore, he set out to change Canada's system of government from the English style, in which Parliament was supreme, to the French style which gives ultimate power to government-appointed judges putting their own political spins upon a rigid unamendable charter.

In his *Memoirs* he used the word "impose" to describe the process: "once we (the Cabinet) had made the decision to impose minority-language education rights, then logically our position had to be to impose the full charter."[11]

I should mention that representative government, and the supremacy of Parliament, will work so long as the principles of individual freedom under limited government are accepted – and defended – by the elected representatives. Laws and judgments that are made in the circumstances of one century are superseded by others that fit the circumstances of later centuries. Thus for Canada's first century the evolutionary common law constituted the framework of our social order. Even the near-dictatorial power of the prime minister's office was subject to the pressures of public opinion and elections.

But to a committed socialist and revolutionary, who said in

retrospect that "we embarked upon an exercise to change the constitution fundamentally," that was precisely why the parliamentary – and evolutionary – system had to be changed.

What would be the point of making fundamental changes to the Constitution if a later Parliament could change it back again?

Thus the 1982 Charter was not only imposed, it was also made virtually unamendable, and Parliament's supremacy was handed over to government- (not Parliament-) appointed judges. Senator Eugene Forsey wrote in *The Globe and Mail*, March 17, 1987: "The fact is that we now have a Constitution so rigid, so hard to amend, that it will be the devil of a job to get anything new of any consequence into it, and the devil of a job getting anything old of any consequence out of it."

Moreover, by its entrenchment of the politics of redistribution (part III – Equalization and Regional Disparities), the Charter delivered Canadians bound hand and foot into a collectivized welfare state in the socialist mode.

Between 1969 and 1984 the federal debt increased tenfold from $20 billion to $200 billion. By 1991, an average prime rate of 10.46 percent had compounded the debt into $400 billion regardless of efforts to control spending.

What Mr. Justice Willard Estey called "an organic change," and UBC Professor Alan Cairns called "a profound wrenching transformation" was imposed from the top down upon a supposedly free people without consulting them either through a general election or a national referendum.

None of this finds its way into Canada's print or electronic media. Articles or letters to the editor that allude to it are as effectively banned by editorial rejection as are similar views from radio and television talk shows whose hosts either shut participants off or ridicule them before hand-picked panels. Macaulay's fourth estate has long ceased to report the news; by selective reporting it controls it.

To Toronto's newspapers, to *Saturday Night* and *Maclean's*, to the CBC, and to most of Canada's print and electronic media, the one hundred and fifty percent revolution was not news at the time, nor is it news now. The unprecedented growth of the state accords with the views and aims of journalists and commentators

[33]

who have shifted the political centre to the left.

In 1973, Watergate was on Canada's front pages, yet Richard Nixon had not subverted the Constitution, he had not required Americans to seek proficiency in a second language if they aspired to work for their federal government, nor had he, an admitted practitioner of deceit, used deception to change the American system of government.

Here, we step back to 1864, when Canada's Fathers of Confederation began to draft what became the BNA Act. Since it would be an act of the British Parliament, and therefore amendable through the usual processes of that Parliament, there was no need to include an amending formula. Amendments of substance that passed in the Canadian Parliament and that affected the division of powers would be sent to Westminster for approval.

The search for an amending formula that would be acceptable to Ottawa and the provincial legislatures began in 1927. The attempt failed, as did a second in 1931, when the Statute of Westminster recognized the independence of self-governing countries of the Commonwealth. Because Canada was unable to agree on an amending formula, it had to ask that the BNA Act be excepted from the Statute. Subsequent attempts in 1935–36, 1950 and 1961 also failed but another in 1964 – the Fulton-Favreau formula – was approved in principle only to be set aside after failure to get unanimous provincial support.

At the Victoria Conference in June 1971, agreement was reached on a formula as part of a wider constitutional package that would have allowed amendment after the constitution had been "patriated" from Westminster. But under pressure from *Le Devoir* editor Claude Ryan, who argued that redistribution of federal powers should precede patriation, Quebec Premier Robert Bourassa withdrew support and the attempt failed.[12]

When the Trudeau Liberals were defeated by Joe Clark's Progressive Conservatives in 1979, Trudeau ascribed his defeat to having "travelled energetically and talked everywhere I went about the constitution."[13] He was defeated, and when a new election was forced after the Clark government lost a motion in the House on its first budget, and on Finance Minister John Crosbie's valiant attempt to restore some fiscal sanity to the federal finances,

Trudeau and his Liberal Party strategists won by campaigning cynically on "Cheap Gas," and were returned to power.

In short, when Trudeau ran on his proposed changes to the Constitution he was defeated. When he ran again on bread and butter promises, he was returned, but without an electoral mandate for fundamental change to the constitution. Nevertheless that was accorded priority and the necessary planning was set in train.

The plan, and the deception that was part and parcel of it, were as ingenious as you might expect from the clever people who did the work. Whatever one's political persuasion, few would question that Michael Pitfield and Michael Kirby, to cite two leading figures, were clever men. But as Colin Campbell wrote during that period: "The departments and agencies of the government of Canada and the key individuals who operate them reflect the preferences of one man to a degree usually attained only in one-party regimes. Certainly, not even the power of appointment of American presidents affords the type of latitude provided by Trudeau's long years in office."[14]

Since Ottawa and the provinces had been unable to agree on an amending formula, and since because of this Ottawa was obliged to send the sort of amendments that the planners had in mind to Westminster for approval, why shouldn't Ottawa simply determine an amending formula, write the formula into a constitutional package that included a Charter of Rights and Freedoms, use the government's majority to force the package through the Canadian Parliament and send the whole thing to Westminster to approve as its final legislative act on Canada's behalf?

The whole deception – the planned overthrow of centuries-old institutions by a handful of political schemers – was breathtaking in its audacity. And it succeeded.

It was not done easily. When the Liberal government invoked closure to force the resolution into the committee stage where eventual passage would be secured by the government's majority in the House, Joe Clark and a number of his MPs rushed the Speaker's chair demanding to be heard. A special joint parliamentary committee was struck, hearings were prolonged over sixty-five days and the first charter was redrafted five times. Court challenges were mounted by eight provinces (Ontario and New

Brunswick supported Ottawa), the Supreme Court ruled in Ottawa's favour (but ruled also that proceeding without provinces' agreement to a reduction in their powers would be a breach of convention), and after a "one last time" conference that lasted four days from November 2, 1981, the deed was done. Quebec Premier René Lévesque, who alone had an electoral mandate to change the Constitution, was absent when the final draft was approved and when it was presented to him the next morning he refused to sign the accord.

This is a good place to describe the mechanics of that "one last time" conference.

There were no parliamentary rules of debate. The Prime Minister set the agenda, and he was in charge. Thus after having been opposed all morning by a majority of the premiers, Mr. Trudeau simply adjourned the meeting for lunch and afterwards went straight to discuss his proposal, clause by clause. Quebec Premier René Lévesque, representing over a quarter of the country's population, became one of eleven equal first ministers.

Quebec's refusal to sign was based on solid ground. Donald Smiley, for over three decades one of Canada's leading scholars and teachers in Canadian political science, regarded the Act as nothing less than a betrayal of Quebec. It was "an integral part of a general initiative from Ottawa towards a more highly centralized federal system...the Charter is inherently a fragmenting rather than a unifying measure...the defence of rights centres on conflict rather than cooperation."[15]

At first sight, successive Quebec governments' rejection of written charters (Victoria in 1971, the Trudeau charter in 1981 and a later idea of a "social" charter) appears to be contradictory. After all, drawing up and abiding by rigid written charters is a French tradition. But written charters are inconsistent with the English tradition of parliamentary supremacy, a tradition that suits Quebec's peculiar ability to dominate Canadian parliaments by the use of its bloc vote.

The BNA Act installed a federal system by defining the exclusive powers of the national and provincial legislatures (sections 91, 92, and 93), but it also recognized, in section 133, the right of French-speaking Canadians to use the French language in parliamentary debates, as well as in the courts, of Canada and Quebec. Privileges, including education, of Roman Catholic subjects were protected by section 93.

Section 133 was a concession to French-speaking subjects, but, like the BNA Act itself, it was part of statute law, and therefore amendable by a parliament. The nub of Canada's constitutional "problem" was failure to agree on an amending formula that would still protect the provincial powers enumerated in section 92, and bound up with that in the case of Quebec was any change to section 133. Quebec's bloc voting power – and its claim to a Quebec veto – may have been used to stymie change but its use of that power was not inconsistent with the parliamentary process.

Thus do we see how, despite Quebec's persistent use of its bloc vote to gain effective control of Parliament, the failure to amend was still a *parliamentary* failure, and therefore roundly constitutional.

It was not so much Pierre Trudeau's aversion to nationalism as his obsession with language, and his passion to put his Official Languages Act beyond the power of a future parliament to change or repeal it, that drove him to change the parliamentary system. He could not stomach the English tradition of parliamentary supremacy, and he contrived to do away with it by two tricks.

The first he described in an address to Liberal party members in Quebec City, October 22, 1980, when he said: "I'll tell you something else: we also wanted to entrench language rights; unfortunately, I think it's true that, if we had done so, we would have seen certain people in the country fighting the project saying, 'there goes that French power government again, which only wants to help and protect francophones.' It was to broaden the debate that we wanted to entrench fundamental rights."[16]

The "organic change" of making the 1982 Charter the supreme law of Canada was achieved by a second trick, an elaborate deception of the Canadian electorate who had not been consulted about constitutional change before Trudeau's election in 1980. The people were not told that the purpose was to subordinate their elected representatives to the ultimate authority of nine government-appointed judges, nor was it explained that this would weaken parliaments' facility for continuous change by means of the case-by-case tradition of the common law. Instead, they were told that the purpose was to "patriate" the Constitution from Canada's colonial masters who had in fact proclaimed Canada's full sovereignty by the Statute of Westminster in 1931.

The deception was not lost on the British Parliament, whose leading constitutional authority, the Right Honourable J. Enoch Powell, spoke to the Canada Bill on March 3, 1982:

> As we go on through the Bill, my fear deepens that we are engaged, largely innocently, in perpetrating a fraud....It is also incompatible with the rule of law, as we understand it, which requires that the law shall be so defined and of such a character that the citizen may reasonably inform himself in advance of what will or will not be adjudged to be lawful. Certainly, no one reading the generalities of the early part of the schedule [the Charter of Rights and Freedoms] could possibly decide how a court would rule upon so many measures which in legislation we are careful by procedure to define as accurately and precisely, and often intelligently, as we can....
>
> My object is to distinguish the two separate things which the Committee is invited to do in the Bill, and to approve one of them and exclude the other. My purpose is to ensure that the Bill patriates to Canada the right to make the constitutional and other law of Canada, removes the constitution from the statute book of this country and removes our hitherto retained right to legislate for Canada. That I describe in a single word – patriation.
>
> The Bill also enacts a charter of rights and constitution for Canada which has not existed before. I believe that the Bill should do the first of those two things and should not do the second....
>
> Somehow the notion has been gained in some quarters in Canada that once the bill has been passed by this Parliament it has an entrenchment, authority, validity and unamendability that it cannot have if it is passed by the Canadian Parliament....I am driven to the unpleasant

conclusion that there has been a deception for the purpose of conveying a misleading impression – that the British Parliament could entrench the provisions, whereas the Canadian Parliament cannot. However, we know that that is not so. At the moment that it sent the Bill to us, the Canadian Parliament said that the purpose of the whole operation was that it was

> "in accord with the status of Canada that Canadians be able to amend their Constitution in Canada in all respects."

That means every jot and tittle of it. They can amend it. Therefore, they have told us that there is nothing that can be entrenched, because they will have the right to amend anything in the constitution....

We are obliged to deduce that the Canadian Government, by inducing the Canadian Parliament to make this request in this form, were engaged in deceiving one or more important interests in Canada about the result of that constitution being placed first on the statute book of Britain and then being patriated to Canada....

It is an unhappy event that we should part from a legislative responsibility that we exercised for our one remaining Dominion under a cloud of incomprehension and misunderstanding and the suspicion that we are being used as a tool to produce political results in Canada that could not have been produced without that form of deception.[17]

(The "inducing" Mr. Powell referred to was effected by the Liberals' invoking closure on the debate in Ottawa.)

Mr. Powell's point about the Charter's being incompatible with the rule of law because citizens would be unable to predict how its many provisions would be interpreted, and the corollary that both law-making and in fact Constitution-making would fall into the hands of judges, has been enlarged upon by Professor Peter Russell. He wrote that the Supreme Court's most important responsibility "is to give some size and shape to the actual rights which these vague phrases are to entail. In discharging this responsibility the Court is performing a constitution-making role which is at least as significant as that performed by the politicians and civil servants who wrote the Charter."[18]

The Charter constitutes Pierre Trudeau's fundamental change from what might be called a negative to a positive concept of the relation between citizen and government.

As Mr. J.P. Nowlan explained in the House of Commons, October 10, 1980: "We are talking about civil law and common law....The whole foundation of this country in nine provinces is that we have all the rights in the world except those that say, 'Stop at a Stop sign, do not drive too fast, do not drink too much and do not kill somebody.' Those are the laws that have restricted the open-ended common law....Under the civil code one does not have any right to do anything unless one can point to it in some constitution, some bill of rights or some charter."

It's not hard to see the effect of the change. In a common law jurisdiction obeying or breaking the law is a matter of individual choice. The law is there. It is understood, and it is up to the citizen to abide by it or risk penalties that are also understood. The whole society is self-regulating. Citizens look upon the courts as places of last resort, where contracting parties who fail to reach agreement turn for a judgment.

But under the civil code, it is government that tries to regulate the society. In the words of Alain Peyrefitte, "Excessive governmental responsibility encourages lack of responsibility in the citizen."[19]

Who can doubt the significance of the change? Not a day passes without the latest demand by this group or that for the "rights" it claims to be entitled to under the Charter. Matters that until the day before yesterday would have been settled not merely out of court but also without either contestant even considering resort to it, are now the bones of contention to be picked over by lawyers in search of fees or who, as government-appointed members of commissions and tribunals, are revelling in their arbitrary powers.

This is as good a place as any to consider what Canada's

revolutionaries have done to "reform" Canadian society since they started the revolution thirty years ago by expanding the state.

The whole thrust of the state's expansion was toward uniformity. The purpose of the state, after all, is to enforce laws which impose restraints upon individual liberty. The purpose of the restraints is to prevent one individual from trespassing upon the liberty of another. The good fences which make good neighbours are policed by the state. Keeping the peace is its one acknowledged duty.

But as the Latin tag attests, who, indeed, guards the guardians? It is that temptation to butt in, to make a nuisance of oneself, which is at the root of the matter. We are prone to it as individuals. In our pride we can see how things might be better ordered, especially as they affect our neighbours. By prodigies of self-control we may refrain from telling them, but the urge is there nevertheless. What holds us back is partly the fear that our advice will be resented but more that it will be ignored. With maturity we learn to suppress these urges, to take people as they come, even to recognize in them shortcomings of our own.

The state, however, is subject to no such impediments. The secret of its power lies in its very remoteness. It is one thing to refrain from advising the man next door, whom we know. It is another thing altogether to compose a set of regulations for people collectively. They are as diverse as the regulations are uniform. Their diversity constitutes a perpetual challenge. If only people would respond to the forecasts, if only the behaviour which is predictable in general terms would conform in particular ones to the trend of the graph.

That is the challenge which the Canadian State felt called upon to meet. It had, its servants came to realize, the power to regulate. Not in order to create wealth, but to regulate the private citizens who were engaged in wealth creation. Dealers in illusion, the state's servants applied themselves to the task with a will. Each fresh set of regulations exposed gaps that must be filled. The establishment of one board revealed the need for a second. Unless it sow the seeds for continuance in another form, no commission of inquiry was complete.

As the regulations mounted, as the boards and commissions

proliferated, the law itself was crushed under the weight of them. Relationships which had been simple were made complex. Rules which everyone could understand were multiplied into abstractions and interpretations and footnotes to sub-sub-paragraphs until they were incomprehensible to everybody, not least the authors, least of all the lawyers and judges whose lives were consumed in deciphering them.

One result was to bring the civil law into contempt. Another was to establish, outside the courts, a court where there were neither lawyers nor judges, where arbitrary rulings were the prerogative of inspectors, regulators, and commissioners, and where mountains of precedent were built upon molehills of law.

When the growth of a bureaucracy passes beyond control, it becomes a law unto itself. The process is self-fulfilling. The failure of each new intrusion compels it to intrude again. More people are hired, more programmes devised to occupy them, until the bureaucracy's original purpose is obscured. No longer is it there to administer the law, for the law has been buried. It is there to minister to itself.

The contempt which this process heaps upon the civil law was conscripted to bring the criminal law into disrepute. Here, however, the attack was mounted from that other bastion of liberalism — permissiveness.

The doctrine that instinct deceives, that behaviour is conditioned by circumstances, and that the failure of individuals to conform to society's rules is not their fault but society's, was applied enthusiastically to the treatment of criminals.

Did he steal? He had been deprived by society. Did he commit crimes of violence? He was the victim of a society which, in its disregard for his needs, was violent to him. Did he commit murder? The pressures that society exerted upon him were too great to be borne.

It was in this that liberalism's fundamental contradiction was fulfilled.

The attitude which dictated a concern for people in general while denying the legitimate aspirations of individuals in particular was reversed when some of those individuals broke the law. Then they were transformed from a condition of individuality to one of membership in a class. Not a criminal class, as our fore-fathers held before the enlightenment, but an underprivileged class, a class which had somehow escaped the welfare net, a class, in consequence, which it was society's duty to rescue.

If members of the class were not responsible for their condition, how could they be blamed, much less punished, for actions that derived from it? Innocent until proved guilty, they must be freed without delay until the crowded calendar could admit their reappearance. In the meantime society would muster its social workers, its psychiatrists, its publicly appointed counsel and its special pleaders to excuse, to explain, by all possible endeavours to exculpate the accused.

The police, whose duty to catch the transgressor was discharged upon his arrest, were witnesses to a process which put them, who defend the law, upon the defensive. By a curious twist of reasoning, the police were the enemy, not the criminal. As the tangible representatives of the society that wronged him, they were clearly in the wrong.

The contradiction culminated in the treatment of premeditated murder. Whether he was a domestic bandit, who killed for money, or an international one who killed for a cause, he must be preserved from the fate he dealt without hesitation to his victims.

The principle of an eye for an eye, which served from Moses' day until recently, was abrogated by those to whom principles were an encumbrance. That the victims were innocent, were in fact strangers until the gun introduced a fleeting intimacy, was ignored. Conveniently, they were dead, members of the largest class of all, and the state had no responsibility for them. It was free to turn its attention to the well-being of their murderer.

Predictably, the word *murderer* was the first casualty. The domestic murderer was never referred to by that term. It was too precise. It admitted of no doubt that he did, with the premeditation which is inseparable from taking a weapon to the scene of his crime, kill someone on purpose. After the event the word was too harsh a reminder of the harshness of his crime.

The welfare state, whose aim was to cushion its wards from the inescapable realities of life and death, must itself escape reality. In court, the domestic murderer became "the accused." When guilt had been established he was thenceforward referred to by name, as befitted his notoriety. If, after the passage of time, he was referred to again, the public's recollection was prompted by reference to the crime he was "involved in." When, in due course, he was released, if the crime were sufficiently newsworthy his earlier notoriety would be revived. The name of his victim might even be mentioned, though not in a reproachful way, because he had now paid his debt to society. The murder he committed had been expunged. It was as if it had never been.

By imputing to the abstraction of society the qualities which could be identified only with the individuals who comprised it, the state, which was itself an abstraction, subverted the truth. Society, which could not be punished, was blamed for the crime which only a person could commit. The theory that no one, because of upbringing or environment or deprivation or whatever, was responsible for anything, required the creation of a substitute. Since reason and instinct told us that there could be no substitute, the state must confound us by indirection.

Like a magician's audience we were led to believe that things were not what they seemed. Society which was to blame in the first place had become the victim of the murderer it bred. When he had paid to it the debt of his crime his unfortunate lapse would be forgotten, swallowed up by abstractions as woolly as the thinking that gave rise to them.

The international bandit could be disguised in more fanciful terms. He was at worst a terrorist, more often a freedom fighter, a nationalist, an urban guerilla, or simply a member of the "movement" of the hour. Never was he a murderer. The people he killed were not the victims of his guns or his grenades or his dynamite, but of the circumstances which drew them to that particular airplane, or embassy, or public place.

They were hostages against the fulfillment of demands in which they had no concern. Secure until that moment in the possession of identity and occupation, they surrendered both to the cause of their assailants. As hostages they would suffer, as hostages they might die, but there was nothing personal about it. The abstractions which served the domestic scene were applied the more easily to the international. For if the public sector at home was out of control, the super-sector that sprouted from the United Nations abroad was out of all reason.

If it was foolish to blame a national society, from which traditional values had been banished, for crimes committed by persons, then transferring that blame to international society, which had neither tradition nor values, merely compounded the folly.

To suppose that, by seconding them to the United Nations, national bureaucrats acquired qualities superior to those of their fellows at home, was only the first in a chain of assumptions. If experience led us to doubt the validity of the domestic assumption – that all wisdom resided in the state and, by implication, in its servants – the sheer impertinence of the international assumption might well leave us breathless. Applying to an international court the same social theories which had brought domestic courts into disrepute was to confuse issues already confounded. The effect was to dissipate responsibility to such an extent that it disappeared.

That the Security Council should be as powerless as the United Nations of which it was part was wholly consistent with the theories that gave birth to them both. That nations which were manifestly unable to govern themselves individually – many having acquired nationhood the day before yesterday – should be credited with the ability to govern all nations collectively, including those with centuries of tradition and cohesion behind them, was the final absurdity. Yet it persists.

The motive force can be ascribed to two distinct impulses. First is the natural tendency of the state to dissolve its responsibility in committees. The drive to escape responsibility, to seek the shelter of a consensus, at all costs to be fireproof, is the inevitable corollary of social theories which hold no one to blame for anything.

The ready assumption of personal responsibility, attributed to George Washington in the matter of the tree and his little hatchet, may be apocryphal, but its survival springs from more than Americans' veneration of their first president. It marks a rare quality. How rare may be judged when we try to recall examples of public figures, whose prompt acceptance of responsibility for deemed successes is a daily occurrence, accepting responsibility for evident failures. "It was my fault" — that, to borrow an American idiom, will be the day.

The second motive is more sinister. The drive to transfer power from the individual to the state — indeed to render the individual powerless — finds its natural extension in the transfer of power from individual nations to the international body that foreshadows the world state.

No doubt all this was within the spirit of the times. Unfortunately for Canada it accorded also with the spirit that moved her home-grown revolutionaries.

Their legacy is a creeping mediocrity that substitutes envy for excellence. The independence which drives men to seek the best is attacked by those who would make all dependent on the state, on the great fiction, as Bastiat put it, by which everybody tries to live at the expense of everybody else.

• FOUR •

The expansion of the federal civil service that began with Lester Pearson's imposition of "universal" medicare and other social programmes, and accompanied by his installation of civil servants' right to strike, was manifested from the mid-1960s onwards in a rash of new government buildings to house the growing numbers. Between 1964 and 1975 the federal civil service grew 65 percent, from 200,000 to 330,000.

Speaking in London, England, January 11, 1977, Canada's Labour Minister John Munro said that Canada would benefit if Canadian unions were stronger, and he "cited the monolithic power of the British union movement as a model that would improve Canadian industrial relations."[1] By that time the Canadian Union of Public Employees (CUPE) was the largest union in Canada, and while union membership in the private sector was about 25 percent of the work force, in the public sector it was soon to exceed 90 percent.[2] Given federal civil servants' entitlement to "free collective bargaining" and the right to strike, the monolithic power was within their grasp and CUPE's research director exhorted them accordingly in the March 1977 issue of *The Labour Gazette*: "Changes in technology are making public service strikes less effective. Public sector unions will find it necessary to turn the screws a little tighter, to stay out on strike a little longer, and to find new techniques if the strike weapon is to remain as effective as it was in the past."

In the private sector, although union members were compelled by law to pay union dues under threat of expulsion and loss of employment, union intransigence was tempered by competition; if Box Inc. was struck, Cox Inc. could still offer its wares.

But members of CUPE and other civil service unions had monopolies of the services they were paid to perform. If air traffic controllers struck, the public didn't fly. If post office employees struck, there was no mail. If school teachers struck, there was no school. If public transport was struck, the public had to walk or thumb rides.

But throughout the strikes, government went on. When the strikes were over, the jobs were still there. The politicians and senior civil servants who did the "bargaining" were still entitled to their pay and fully indexed pensions.

Now, two monopolies, the state and its employees, were joined against their nominal employer, the citizens of Canada, and in the manner of monopolies, both of them expanded. Burgeoning social programmes, state-subsidization of advocacy groups, grants and subsidies to business and industry, transfer payments to individuals and regions in the sacred cause of equalization – Canada had become the proving ground for redistributionist politics on the grand scale. And as union monopolies in the public sector extorted pay and benefit raises unconnected to productivity, so did private sector unions use the strike weapon to get "parity" with the public sector. And much of the welfare state's expense was funded with borrowed money.

In 1969, the last year of a balanced federal budget, and after a century that included two world wars, the federal debt was about $20 billion. By 1984, after fifteen years of peace during which spending on national defence had declined from 20 percent to 10 percent of the total, the deficit was $38 billion (54 percent of revenues) and the debt was $200 billion.[3]

Socialism was in full flower. It remained to secure the garden against future intruders, but this time it was done by a trick, with a brush of the hand to the democratic form.

Here we come to the fundamental truth of Canadian politics. Quebec votes en bloc for the party it thinks is going to win, and no party can win a majority unless it wins the Quebec vote.

From Confederation in 1867 until 1984, with only seven exceptions, Quebecers voted solidly for one party. Until 1984 and 1988, when Brian Mulroney won Quebec for the Tories, the total Quebec vote in all thirty-four elections had been over three to one for the Liberals.

Quebecers' attitude has been to go with the assumed winner, first with Sir John A. Macdonald/Sir George-Étienne Cartier, then, after the Riel affair, with the Liberal Party that bribed Quebec and divided English Canada.

It was in 1891, post-Riel, that the Conservative majority in Quebec disappeared. A century later in the 1993 election, the Bloc Québécois sank the Liberals in Quebec but the principle (if you can call it that) was unchanged: vote for the winner that will get the best deal for Quebec. In 1993 also there was a new bonus: assurance of a Prime Minister from Quebec (however unpopular there), and a solid Bloc speaking only for Quebec.

Yet the federal system suits Quebec, and for this reason. Just as the French tradition of top-down government predisposes Quebecers to centralized authority within the province, so must they resist attempts by the federal government to invade their provincial government's authority. They use their bloc vote to secure redistributions from Ottawa, while resisting the intrusion of Ottawa's political power that redistribution entails. Thus Trudeau's centralization of power in Ottawa added fuel to the fire of the separatists.

His two obsessions were bilingualism and the Constitution. He thought that by spreading the use of French across the country Quebec's nationalism would die on the vine. But he couldn't protect his language policy against amendment or repeal by a later parliament because it was only statute law, and in the British parliamentary tradition, parliament was supreme. So he had to change the Constitution, and it was done by a trick.

He did it by claiming to "patriate" the Constitution from Westminster, which had proclaimed Canada's sovereignty in 1931, and inveigling the British Parliament into passing a Canada Bill with a built-in Charter of Rights and Freedoms that incorporated his language legislation and an amending formula that made the Constitution almost unamendable.

The deception, imposed upon a nominally free people, changed Canada's system of government from its foundation in the evolutionary common law, in which individuals exercised their inherent freedom to abstain from doing what the law prohibited, to a system where their "Rights" and "Freedoms" were no longer inherent; they were written down and "Guaranteed" by the state, that is, they would be vulnerable to whatever meaning the state or its courts decided to give them.

In 1981, former Supreme Court of Canada chief justice the

Right Honourable Bora Laskin said: "After the Canadian Bill of Rights we had twenty years of good jurisprudence. I predict that after the proposed Charter of Rights and Freedoms we will have fifty years of dissent."[4]

In June 1982, former clerk to the Privy Council Gordon Robertson wrote: "Our 'patriated' Constitution contains no reflection of any of the demands that had been put forward by Quebec governments to meet dissatisfaction in that province.

"It is quite possible that the leaders and people of Quebec may turn their attention to more urgent things and leave the Constitution aside for some time to come. However, it would be dangerous to believe that the issue is settled. Indeed, the Conference of 1981 and the 'patriation' of 1982 may well create an array of new grievances that, over time, could become a mythology of betrayal, isolation, and imposition. There probably was no better alternative in the circumstances, but the fact remains that the elected government of Quebec was isolated and alone in November 1981. It is also a fact that both the Charter of Rights and the new amending formula were 'imposed.'"[5]

Since 1982, as Bora Laskin predicted, Canada has become a nation of litigants wherein state-subsidized groups of every description have elbowed their way toward whatever benefits their lawyers can winkle out for them from the Charter.

Affirmative action programmes, official bilingualism and official multiculturalism, equalization payments between individuals and regions – the whole panoply of state intervention into private and business life was embedded in the country's fundamental law. The garden gate was locked and bolted.

To attribute Trudeau's successful insinuation of socialism to his prior imposition of official bilingualism may appear at first glance to be stretching a point. But we have to remember that we are dealing with a consummate political strategist, who called Mao Tse-tung "that superb strategist" and thought that Chairman Mao's experience "might lead us to conclude that in a vast and heterogeneous country, the possibility of establishing socialist strongholds in certain regions is the very best thing."[6]

Also, as Professor John Saywell remarked in his introduction to the English edition of Trudeau's essays, *Federalism and the French*

Canadians, "Consistency is, in fact, the most remarkable quality of Mr. Trudeau's thoughts and actions over the past two decades."[7] That was in 1968, the year Mr. Trudeau began his long reign, and I believe it supplies the clue to his success. That the consistency still applied twenty-four years later was evidenced when, in process of working with Brian McKenna to produce a carefully staged version of his memoirs, Trudeau went again to see his friend Fidel Castro. Brian McKenna described the trip in a *Saturday Night* article, December 1993, entitled "Comrades-in-Arms" which included these excerpts: "Trudeau is delighted to discover that Samuel de Champlain designed Havana's harbour. There is also a statue to the French-Canadian explorer Pierre Le Moyne d'Iberville, who died of fever in Havana in 1706. 'French-Canadian tourists have been coming to Havana for a long time,' I remark to Trudeau. He laughs. This is one of his favourite themes, that French Canadians should look beyond the borders of Quebec to the world explored and conquered by ancestors such as Champlain and d'Iberville. 'Why settle for Quebec when you can run all of Canada, before taking on the world?'

"They greet each other with an embrace, like two ageing Catholic cardinals...Trudeau asks Castro about the disappearance of Communism in the world. 'Pierre, it's a tragedy. For poor countries the results are horrific...socialists found ways to moderate the pain brought by the capitalist system...now the situation is horrible for the Third World.'"

Reviewing the filmed *Memoirs*, which he described as being "more successful for his [Trudeau's] purpose than his largely ghost-written book," historian Desmond Morton wrote: "Consider the Canada he inherited in 1968: richer per capita than its American neighbour, troubled by regional differences and disparities but self-assured enough to give its heart to a philosopher. Compare with Canada at the end of Trudeau's term: divided, deficit-ridden and dropping, in per capita income, below half a dozen European countries. In 1968, Quebec separatism was a threat; western alienation was a chronic eccentricity. By 1984, the Parti Québécois was in power and the country was desperate enough to accept Brian Mulroney."[8]

Ralph Waldo Emerson wrote that "A foolish consistency is

the hobgoblin of little minds." Trudeau's was hardly a little mind, but in his politics he showed a consistency that was tragic for Canada. Still, in his old age, consorting with the Cuban communist dictator, still bemused by his failure to resolve the contradiction between his, I believe genuine, concern for individual freedom, and his fascination with the grand solutions that Colin Campbell called a "profound commitment to development of government machinery" and "instituting or expanding central agencies" which nibbled away relentlessly at that freedom; still, in short, the socialist he had been when the Liberal Party, and a majority of Canadians, chose him to lead them in 1968 — consistency drove him as he drove his country.

When Richard Gwyn wrote in *The Northern Magus* that official bilingualism "was nothing less than a social revolution," he was referring to "fundamental changes in Canada's power structure" and the way language policy shot an elite group of "upper middle-class francophones and those upper middle-class anglophones, most from Montreal, who by the happenstance of their parents or their career patterns, had a chance while young to learn French" to the topmost branches of Canada's political power tree. But Gwyn also described them as being "often insufferably self-righteous" because bilingualism had come to them so naturally.

It is a truism to say that self-righteousness and socialism are intertwined. The assumption of moral superiority, the missionary zeal to set the world to rights, the conviction that imperfect man is perfectible if only he can be made to follow socialists' instructions for collective behaviour: these are the traits that lie at the root of terrible events in this century.

Link those traits to the power of a Canadian prime minister's office, distribute them through the inhabitants of the power structure while implementing a policy to which they instinctively adhere, a policy that is lent the appearance of being "equitable" and "holding the country together," and you have the vital elements for establishing socialist strongholds in certain regions of this vast and heterogeneous country.

This is not to say that the implementors of the policy, who ranged from MPs through senior bureaucrats to the presidents, staffs, and members of the hundreds of francophone associations across the country, were or even regarded themselves as being socialists. Rather did they constitute reception areas for federal and provincial government funds that were destined to spread the use of French and by that apparently innocent means to create all the structural appurtenances – government departments, school boards and schools and colleges, community centres and trade associations, labels and road signs, translators and "animators" – of the redistributionist politics that is socialism's raison d'être. They, the government-subsidized francophone associations, were the pioneers on the road to socialism. On that road, the signs read "Entitlement," "Equality," and "Rights"; governments' services and programmes are regarded as "free," and no one speaks of duties or responsibilities.

By 1981, when the wording of the Charter had been hammered out, among its inconsistencies and contradictions was the beguilingly innocent statement (16 [3]) that "Nothing in this Charter limits the authority of Parliament or a legislature to advance the equality of status or use of English or French."

Imagine yourself, a francophone by birth, as the civil servant in charge of French language services in one of the eight English-speaking provinces (New Brunswick is officially bilingual, Quebec unilingually French). Let us say it is Saskatchewan, where census-takers divide the population of just over a million into three linguistic categories by their mother tongues: English, French, and Other. Respectively, the percentages are 81.9, 2.3, and 15.7, and they represent, in the same order, 827,250; 23,720; and 158,655 people (1986 Census).

You have at your disposal a budget to advance the equality of status or use of French to that of English, a daunting task but one in which the Secretary of State for Canada hands out about $23 million under the programme "Support to Official Language Communities." In Saskatchewan no fewer than seventy-nine associations are funded whose sole purpose is to advance, by their various means, the use of French in Saskatchewan. In money power they range from the Comité Fransaskois de St. Front with its paltry $500 allotment, to the mighty Association Culturelle Franco-Canadienne de la Saskatchewan and its $616,281 (1990-91 figures).[9]

Altogether, those seventy-nine associations muster $3,698,057 of federal government funds, or $155.90 for every mother-tongue

French speaker in the province. Each association has its officials, some no doubt voluntary but many more paid full-time. They are your support staff, the advisers you can depend upon for ammunition when budget-making time comes around. Your job has all the marks of bureaucratic perfection. It is not merely self-perpetuating, because its justification is embedded in the supreme law of Canada, it is self-expanding too. For however distressing it may be to francophones – and indeed to francophiles – their share of the provincial population has fallen dramatically since 1941, from 4.9 percent to 2.3. While in those forty-five years the province's English-speakers increased 65 percent, from 499,925 to 827,250, its French-speakers declined by 45 percent, from 43,728 to 23,720.[10] Clearly the task calls for more funds, even for more staff. If French is to be advanced to equality of status or use with English, there is much to be done.

You remember reading about Ontario, where 3 percent of the population speaks French in the home, and where impressive results have been achieved.[11] Although that much richer and more populous province gets about the same amount of money as Saskatchewan from the Secretary of State ($4,097,744 vs. your $3,698,057) for its 113 francophone associations, it has a four-million-dollar Office of Francophone Affairs and, for a dozen years now, a French Language Services Act that generated, in 1990 alone, no less than $315 millions of spending on French language services in twenty-five ministries or agencies, while receiving another $68 million from Ottawa as an Education Grant. On further inquiry you find that Ontario has not only built and established facilities *for* francophones, it has also expanded the French presence by making some of the facilities – community centres, colleges, hospitals – available only *to* francophones. Immigrants to Ontario from French-speaking countries are specially considered for provincial government jobs, and grants are available to help them set up French-language newspapers for their communities. Ontario has subsidized a directory of French-language companies so that they can deal with one another and be identified for government contracts, and has advertised in Quebec and New Brunswick newspapers for French-speaking people to fill the government-created "bilingual" jobs in Ontario's schools and police forces. Above all, Ontario has spent millions of dollars advertising in French-language newspapers urging readers to demand service in French. These last, the "animators," are the shock troops of change, the activists who delight in making nuisances of themselves, all at the public expense.

Repeat this experience in the other seven English-speaking provinces, and we see how the socialist method, the gradual expansion of the state and its agencies into private and commercial life, fitted official language policy like a glove.

In short, the method by which Canada was to be made "irreversibly bilingual" was the tool that came naturally into the hand of the man who wrote, in the essay quoted before, "Federalism must be welcomed as a valuable tool which permits dynamic parties to plant socialist governments in certain provinces, from which the seed of radicalism can slowly spread."[12]

The inseparable component of socialism that Trudeau epitomized was the centralization of political power. That he was able to subvert a federal state, which by definition is a place of divided powers, into a welfare state in the socialist mode, is as fitting a memorial as he is likely to get. It betokens both his consistency and his political brilliance, for he proved himself able to do what the Constitution had denied him – and changed the Constitution in the process.

Two of his lieutenants, Jean Chrétien and Serge Joyal, deserve a mention here. On October 6, 1980, in the House of Commons, then justice minister Jean Chrétien said:

> English and French will be entrenched as the official languages of Canada....I said in Quebec that I had a mandate from my caucus and from my cabinet to state that we will change Canada...we are committed to continue the renewal of our constitution, to review the division of power, to change Canadian institutions.

In a speech to the Acadian Federation of Nova Scotia, November 13, 1982, then secretary of state Serge Joyal said:

> Everything we undertake and everything we are doing to make Canada a French state is part of a venture I have

shared for many years with a number of people...the primary reason why I supported and intervened directly in the patriation of the Constitution, because it offered permanent entrenchment, for as long as God permits this country to exist, of equality of status for French and English in Canadian institutions.

While English Canada slept, and its nominal leader Ontario premier William Davis played his obsequious part in the pre-patriation discussions ("Yes, prime minister"), the march to a language-driven socialist state pressed on relentlessly. Within ten years after the Constitution was changed, the Secretary of State was handing $23 million dollars a year to 396 "Official Language Communities," of which eighteen were anglophone (two federal and the rest in Quebec) and 378 francophone (113 of them in Ontario). Yet according to the 1991 Census, there were only 151,000 French speakers outside Quebec who were unable to speak English. In his book *Lament For A Notion*, author Scott Reid estimated that the total cumulative cost of federal languages policy has been "the addition of 49 billion to the federal debt, billions more to various provincial debts, and a permanent loss to Canadian consumers [associated with regulatory compliance with the *Consumer Packaging and Labelling Act*] of 40 billion worth of consumption." Yet west of the Ontario-Manitoba border only 5,430 francophones were unable to conduct a conversation in English, and "Among those of school age and working age, only 2,195 individuals in all of Western Canada were capable of speaking French but not English."[13]

The man who regarded Mao Tse-tung as "that superb strategist" merely applied Mao's strategy to the vast heterogeneous country of Canada, but with this difference: that "the establishment of socialist strongholds in certain provinces, from which the seed of radicalism can slowly spread" was to be reinforced by establishing francophone enclaves wherever French could be shown to have some claim, however tenuous, to survival. ("Why settle for Quebec when you can run all of Canada, before taking on the world?") His French affinity for the centralized political power that is also a requirement of socialism led him naturally to apply the power he had centralized in the cause of establishing like-minded strong-holds across the country. Funded with federal, and some provincial, money, the permanent staffs of francophone associations set about their business of applying the socialist strategy: demand from government the material rewards to suit their aspirations, in this case the establishment of francophone schools and school boards, francophone print and electronic outlets, francophone provincial departments and civil servants, and overall, francophone quotas in all federal institutions everywhere.

As Trudeau's predilection for "creating new central agencies" spread the federal presence, so did it spread the francophone quotas in his expanding State. To ensure that the new colonizers would never lack recruits, a "francobank" was established in which volunteers were deposited, on full pay and allowances, until posts could be found for them either in federal or provincial institutions, or in the francophone associations that were sowing the seeds of radicalism.

And what was English Canadians' response to this monumental skulduggery? At first disbelief, followed by sporadic and unavailing protests to federal and provincial MPs who with half a dozen exceptions toed a party line that mirrored Trudeau's, Chrétien's and Joyal's. Quebec's official language Bill 101, which made Quebec officially unilingual, and which became law in 1977, drew no objection from the federal parties. It was reinforced by a French language office and a surveillance commission, none of whose staff members could be prosecuted for acts connected with their official duties. The identity of any complainant to either of those offices (for a breach of the law) would be protected. Offenders were liable to fines up to $500 for each offence by an individual, and up to $1,000 for companies, increased for subsequent offences to maximums of $1,000 and $5,000 respectively. For each day an offending company failed to "francize" its name, business publications, signs, and advertising, it would be liable, in addition to costs, to a fine of $100 to $2,000.

So pervasive was the myth of anglophone guilt, so comprehensive was anglo politicians' suppression of their constituents' concerns, and so determined were anglo print and electronic media to stigmatize objectors as rednecks and bigots, even fascists, that English Canada was reduced to forming voluntary groups whose protests were routinely stigmatized in the same way. In September 1977 after Irene Hilchie, a federal civil servant in Halifax, Nova Scotia, had seen at first hand the hiring of francophones for manufactured "bilingual" positions, she formed the Alliance for the Preservation of English in Canada (APEC). It grew steadily until at Irene's urging the national office was moved to Toronto and Ronald Leitch, a founding member, assumed the presidency. He and his wife Pauline joined Irene Hilchie's fight when it was patent that no anglo political leader had the guts to speak up for their concerns. APEC issues a monthly newsletter that provides its supporters with facts and comment upon the topic, central to Canada's condition, that is consistently ignored by its print and electronic media (the information about Ontario's French Languages Services Act, quoted above, was published in APEC's newsletter of March 1994). By 1993, when the Charlottetown Accord was put to the people in a national referendum and for the first time Canadians were allowed to vote directly on policies imposed on them since the 1960s, APEC had members in all provinces and a total membership of over 40,000.

Nor was the media's reaction limited to vilification of APEC and other anglo groups. So great was its members' sense of communal guilt that Quebecers must be hailed at every opportunity as a helpless minority striving to throw off the yoke of their 200 years of injustice. Thus the CBC contrived, through a programme called "The Brockville Incident," to blow up a protest, in Brockville, Ontario, by four or five disenchanted anglos (none of them members of APEC) into an anti-French summation of English Canada's attitude. I watched the programme and made notes.

It was shown, November 6 and 7, 1990, on the CBC's *Journal*. A two-part item, both parts were of about thirty minutes air time, and both were similar in content. That is, although the clips shown on the second night were arranged somewhat differently, the content was chiefly a repeat of what was shown the night before. Both parts were repeated on *Newsworld* November 8 and 9, for a total showing of four times in five days.

Since the topic, desecration by a small group of people in September 1989 – more than a year before – of a Quebec flag was inherently inflammatory, I could not understand (a) why the programme was shown at all, and (b) why it was shown twice.

The declared purpose was to track down the four people who first trampled on, then (one person only) spat upon, and (two people) finally set fire to a Quebec flag, a TV clip lasting ten seconds. It transpired that two of them – a husband and wife – had returned to Canada after an absence of twenty years, were very disturbed by the changes that had taken place, particularly as regards the spread of francophone influence in the federal and Ontario governments, and decided to join in the demonstration as their form of protest. A third, a man, had left Quebec because of its language laws. Bilingual himself, his office was raided by the language police on information that he had published a catalogue in English only. The fourth, a native of Quebec, felt he was treated unjustly and personally insulted by Quebec's superior court justices in the course of his divorce proceedings.

Although these points were made, they were overshadowed by the many clips of *the effect* of the flag trampling. (The incident was first broadcast in Ontario when it happened in September 1989, but there was no reaction until March 1990, when the ten-second clip was resurrected and shown by TV stations in Quebec, played and replayed to saturation, and repeated by *Le Point*. According to *The Journal*, at least 60 percent of Quebecers had by then seen the clip.)

Thus "The Brockville Incident" showed visual repeats of the "trampling" clip as they appeared, *after* the Quebec media's resurrection of the story, on Canadian, U.S., and other foreign networks.

There were interviews with Quebec print and electronic journalists as well as short clips of Quebec citizens expressing anger; a longer clip of a prominent Québécoise singing about the indignity heaped by English Canada on the flag (including the too-familiar phrase "We will not forget"); wide-angle shots of the singer's audience, and of masses of Quebec flags and blue and white balloons – evidently a widespread emotional outburst directed *at* an English Canada supposedly united in its hostility to Quebecers.

Missing from the two broadcasts, apart from the two overshadowed statements of grievance, and except for another protester's display of two photographs showing the Canadian flag being burned in Quebec, was any evidence of actions by Quebecers or their government that might lead to hostility among English Canadians. Even the man's account of harassment by Quebec's language police was allowed to be contradicted by an anonymous spokesman for the Commission de Surveillance, who denied that the man could have been charged for his offence, when any listener acquainted with the Offences and Penalties provisions of Bill 101 knew that they were entirely consistent with what the man said. Yet *The Journal* chose to let that denial pass unchallenged.

The producers chose to drag in the vote, by Sault Ste. Marie's Council, that required all *Council* business to be conducted in English. This was the direct result of a number of events: first, the cutting back of transfer payments by Ottawa to the Ontario government; second, the consequent cutbacks in provincial transfers to municipalities; third, new responsibilities, without provincial funding, imposed on municipalities by the province; and fourth, the passage of Ontario's Bill 8, requiring a further expansion of French-language services in the province. The last straw for Sault Ste. Marie's Council was the demand by parents of fifty-three French-speaking students at the French-language separate school (after the school proposed to admit English-speaking students) that Council authorize construction of two new French-language schools: a public school, and a high school as part of a French cultural centre, at a total cost to the municipality of $10 million.

None of this was mentioned by *The Journal*, which pictured Sault Ste. Marie as a typical community of English Canada; anti-French language and anti-Quebec.

Missing, too, was any example of Quebecers' hostility towards English Canada or English-speaking Canadians generally, or towards English-speaking Canadians *in Quebec*. No shots of the fire-bombing of a Zeller's store that dared to show a sign in English as well as the obligatory French; or (except for the photos mentioned above) of repeated burnings of the Canadian flag, including dragging one behind a car; or of Allan Singer's lone fight in defence of his inherent right (denied by the Quebec Government) to use his own language on his own storefront; or of daily indignities heaped upon English-speaking Quebecers.

If the purpose of these broadcasts was to show any French-speaking Quebecers who might happen to be watching *The Journal* instead of *Le Point*, or later watching *Newsworld* in English, why their provincial flag was trampled on, it clearly failed, for there was no attempt to examine underlying causes of the protest. It could not fail, however, to inflame Quebecers' media-fed feeling of English Canada's implacable hostility toward them. (As I write, four years later, Brockville's flag burning still crops up in articles and news reports as the ready-to-hand expression for anglo extremism.)

That *The Journal* should have chosen to aggravate an already bitter mood between the country's two main language groups was curious to say the least. That it should do so just when commissions of the federal and Quebec governments were seeking views on the country's future from Canadians who could be assumed to have seen the broadcasts, was, to other than believers in conspiracy theory, inexplicable.

A lone spokesman, *Gazette* columnist William Johnson, wrote about the National Film Board's activities in Quebec (*Toronto Star*, November 20, 1992), that "the federal agency loves films which celebrate separatism, stimulate a paranoid fear of French disappearing, or wax lyrical over suppressing English in Quebec....But a film which tells the story of the disintegration of Montreal's English-speaking community as a result of Bill 101? Now, wait a minute! We have lived through perhaps the greatest social revolution in Canadian history in the years since 1976, when the Parti Québécois took power. Within a decade, 202,113 English-speaking Quebecers had left — an exodus unparalleled since the deportation of the Acadians....Where was the film board while this was happening, with its mandate to 'interpret Canada to Canadians and to other nations'?" Johnson quoted Concordia University political scientist Maria Peluso, who explained why perfectly bilingual youths were leaving Quebec: "Last year 256 anglophones applied for jobs in the Quebec public sector. And yet only six were hired. So whether you speak French or not is really not an issue. The point is that you're not French. The point is that you're not de souche Québécoise."

It's hardly news (I wrote in a letter to the CRTC) that Canada has become a litigious, fractious society. What *would* be news would be a serious attempt by the CBC to examine the politically inspired causes of our national malaise, rather than exacerbating passions over an isolated English-French incident.

Thus might the CBC embark upon a Brockville Revisited in which the *Canadian* flag burners would be tracked down and interviewed, in which Ontarians concerned about the ramifications of Bill 8 (the proximate cause of the Brockville protest) were also interviewed, and in which English-speaking Quebecers might have equal time to relate their experiences.

How could French-speaking Quebecers form an opinion of English Canada's attitudes when their eyes and ears were bombarded with a single, extreme incident? This was not news, it was propaganda.

Four years later, audiences were permitted to see a partial, belated, and privately initiated response. What Johnson had been referring to in his *Gazette* article was William Weintraub's struggle to get his film about the anglo exodus accepted by the National Film Board. The following year Weintraub was successful and it was issued in video under the title *The Rise and Fall of English Montreal*. It was described on the video case as follows:

> In 1992 Montreal was celebrating its 350th birthday, taking great pride in its beauty and its unique history. But at the same time, thousands of young people were moving away from the city, to make their lives elsewhere.
>
> They were the latest wave in one of the great migrations of Canadian history. In the past twenty years, some 300,000 English-speaking people had left Montreal, convinced that they had no future in a Quebec that was increasingly French, increasingly nationalistic.
>
> In **The Rise and Fall of English Montreal** we meet some of the people who are moving away. The film also recalls the days, in the last century, when there were more English-speaking people than French in Montreal. And it asks whether the Anglo community's great contribution to the life of Montreal, and to the growth of Canada, might some day be completely forgotten.

In November 1994 we ran the video at home and found it a

faithful report of the city where we lived for thirteen years, where our three children were educated, which they left in turn after graduating from McGill, and which we too left in 1971 under the same impetus that caused the exodus: manifestly we were no longer welcome.

I wrote to the CBC's Executive Director of News, Current Affairs, and *Newsworld* (Robert Culbert) to ask if the film had been shown on national television. He replied: "It has not been shown on the CBC. It was screened by the Documentary Unit some considerable time back. The film did not make its way to the list of 20 or so new documentaries that we are able to show each season. We receive literally hundreds of films and suggestions each year. A process of admittedly rough justice gets that number down to the relatively few we can program. Unfortunately, not everyone's favourite film manages to get on the air.

"I am glad you enjoyed the film. It obviously strikes cords [sic] with a number of English Speaking Quebecers, both current and ex-."

At the same time I wrote to TVOntario, whose spokeswoman (Diana Cloud) replied: "I have checked with the Current Affairs Documentary Unit, who would be most likely to program the film. It eventuates that they have indeed considered it for acquisition, but did not find it suitable for inclusion in the schedule."

Also in November 1994, after CBC and TVOntario had turned the film down, I wrote to CTV, suggesting that the topic might be suitable for the investigative programme W5. Five months later CTV thanked me for the suggestion but "don't plan to pursue your story idea."

The film was shown on the Vision Channel, January 14, 1995, in prime time, but readers of the *Globe* were not told about it beforehand: the paper's TV guide showed merely the generic programme spot where it was to appear, *The Cutting Edge*. Nor was it mentioned elsewhere in the paper. But the *Toronto Star* did tell its readers the day before, when historian Michael Bliss referred to it in his column ("And if you want to see some of the sad consequences of thirty years of cultural self-abuse in Quebec, watch the controversial documentary..."), and TV critic Greg Quill did the same ("The [film] is a fascinating, if affectionately one-sided National

Film Board chronicle of a once great city forced into decline by nationalist Quebec sentiments and perverse language laws that have forced thousands of English-speaking Montrealers to flee in the past 20 years"). The *Star* also described the programme in its TV guide ("Montreal celebrates its 350th birthday in 1992").

Three months later, April 17, 1995, when the film was shown on PBS (!), the *Globe*'s television critic John Haslett Cuff wrote: "William Weintraub's informative and provocative documentary should be required viewing for everyone in Canada, but it's had a difficult time even finding a broadcaster. However inflammatory it may seem, it remains a much-needed antidote to the revisionist dishonesty and tiresomely self-serving buffoonery of Quebec's politicians *du jour* who predominate in the mainstream French- and English-language media."

This partial, belated, and privately initiated account of the results from a provincial government's exercise of arbitrary power (and by implication the federal government's abdication of its duty to intervene), "did not make its way" to the CBC's national and *Newsworld* programmes that had given "The Brockville Incident" such prominence four years earlier, but the same mischievous spirit that prompted Brockville's subsequent repetition in Quebec was still at work.

As part of attempts to curb federal spending in 1994, the Chrétien government ordered cutbacks in the Defence budget which included the closing of le Collège militaire royal de Saint-Jean in Quebec and Royal Roads Military College in British Columbia. The Saint-Jean closing was seized by the Bloc Québécois as a stick to beat the sovereigntist drum, and the government's plan to train all officer cadets at Kingston's Royal Military College was condemned accordingly. In the *Toronto Star*'s television guide of the week January 7–14, 1995, critic Peter Trueman reported that the producers of the CBC French network's *Le Point* programme sent a team to Kingston to tape portions of a story about the impact of the closing. He wrote:

> Nancy Drew, who manages a Kingston clothing store, cheerfully invited the *Le Point* crew into her shop when they told her, in English, that they were taping a day in

the life of an RMC cadet. When the camera was rolling, however, the cadet began speaking to Drew in French, and asked for help in selecting a toque.

Caught off guard, the store manager heard herself saying: "I'm sorry, I can't speak French. Could you speak to me in English?"

Understandably, Drew figures she was set up, and is resentful. She said that if the camera hadn't been running she'd have managed the usual way, with good will and her high school French.

Trueman commented that the *Le Point* crew "made an actor out of a cadet, and turned a segment of information programming into soap opera."

Reginald Bibby, the author and sociology professor at the University of Lethbridge, was quoted in *Maclean's* January 6, 1992: "Bilingualism has always been a very reluctant concession to Quebec. Out West, when it is not known whether Quebec is even going to stay in the country, the idea of two official languages becomes almost absurd."

Yet as late as April 22, 1994, "Canada's National Newspaper" was still editorializing in defence of the policy that was rejected almost universally, stated disingenuously that "Bilingualism is required for only 3.3 percent of the federal public service jobs in Western Canada" while omitting any reference to the totally disproportionate percentages of francophones in the upper ranks of the public service, and concluded that the whole business was "Simple, straightforward, fair."

That Canada has become a litigious, fractious society is the direct consequence of Mr. Trudeau's obsession with language policy, of his resulting compulsion to entrench that policy in a radically changed Constitution, and of that new Constitution's embodiment of the collectivist ideas that mark the socialism he espoused all his adult life.

That socialism has been clearly acceptable to the body of media opinion has been as tragic for Canada as the Trudeau revolution itself. First challenging, then disabusing ourselves of those views is a task for the 1990s and beyond.

• FIVE •

Section 27 of the Charter of Rights and Freedoms requires that the Charter "be interpreted in a manner consistent with the preservation and enhancement of the multicultural heritage of Canadians."

Many things could be said about that curious statement. One that seems particularly fitting was part of a contribution by University of Montreal Professor Guy Rocher to the Second Canadian Conference on Multiculturalism, held in Ottawa February 13-15, 1976. Professor Rocher deplored the Trudeau government's plan to separate bilingualism from biculturalism since it betrayed all the hopes French-Canadians might have placed in bilingualism, as they conceived it – "that is, clearly tied to its symbol and essential condition, biculturalism."

It seemed to Professor Rocher that there was an admission of failure in the government's stance – the tacit recognition that there was no Canadian culture, whether English or French. "Whereas a bicultural Canada implies a certain internal cultural structure, a multicultural Canada is the absence of a national culture. What kind of nation, I wonder, can really exist on such a weak and unprepossessing base? I, for one, know of no historical precedent for nationhood founded on the concept of a mini-United Nations, as the Trudeau government is proposing."

Professor Rocher concluded by saying that "to a French-speaking Quebecker, Canada has been and remains an ambiguous country. Nor will the recently discovered multiculturalism make his place in the Canadian mosaic happier and more serene."

Who could argue with that? Obviously Mr. Trudeau did. Five years before in the House of Commons (p. 8545), he had announced "A policy of multiculturalism within a bilingual framework....The government will support and encourage the various cultures and ethnic groups that give structure and vitality to our society."

No doubt all of us are prisoners of birth and heritage. No

doubt my own view of Canadians was stamped by the many I met in England during the years of RAF service before I was posted to Canada as an instructor in August 1939. They had made their way to England on the chance of being awarded short service commissions as pilots in the expanding service and they exhibited the qualities you might expect in young men who had the guts and initiative to work their passages on such a chance. That is to say, they were courageous, physically fit, and well educated. But besides those requisite qualities they had others that were sufficiently widespread to strike me as characteristic of Canadians: polite, but blunt when necessary; practical and down to earth; independent yet ready to help (but not to interfere); not class conscious. When later I came to Canada, those characteristics were confirmed for me in the Royal Canadian Air Force, at the time as ill-equipped in hardware as it was well-equipped in the human material that every military formation in history has depended on for success.

We shared if not birth then certainly heritage. Many had attended professional courses in England. At school and university they had read British history. With allusions to English literature we were on common ground; we sang the same songs, laughed at the same jokes. Was this a bad thing? Was the British tradition of parliamentary government and individual freedom under the evolutionary common law something to be ashamed of and set aside? Lester Pearson thought so. Angus MacLean, a former premier of Prince Edward Island said that Pearson "had a real obsession that you had to sanitize yourself as a country from anything that was British or traditional. A lot of people think that Trudeau started that, but it was Pearson."[1]

If it was Pearson, he started a move that Pierre Trudeau found easy to follow. What Professor Kenneth McRoberts called "his consuming aversion to Quebec nationalism which had brought him to Ottawa in the first place"[2] was of a piece with his aversion to nationalism in general. In a *Cité libre* essay published in April 1962, he had written that nations "belong to a transitional period in world history," that if Canada's two main ethnic and linguistic groups "will collaborate at the hub of a truly pluralistic state, Canada could become the envied seat of a form of federalism that belongs to tomorrow's world....Canadian federalism is an experiment of major proportions; it could become a brilliant prototype for the molding of tomorrow's civilization."[3] Nationalism was out, Canada's new role as the prototype for tomorrow's federation of the world was in.

This brings us back to Mr. Trudeau's two obsessions: the Constitution and bilingualism. The Pearsonian myth of two founding peoples and the Trudeauvian imposition of two official languages sat not at all well with the one-third of Canadians who were of neither British nor French extraction. At the strokes of two pens they had disappeared from the official record. If the two official languages were to have equality of status and equal rights and privileges as to their use in all institutions of the Parliament and government of Canada, the one-third of Canadians classified as "Other" had suddenly become not even second class, but third class citizens behind the co-equal first two.

Then again, apart from a shared lack of English or French backgrounds, "they" were not an identifiable class, but a miscellany of immigrants or descendants of immigrants from Russia, Ukraine, Europe, and Scandinavia, some of them via the United States. In short, even if Professor Rocher's wish for linking language to culture had been met, the problem that now faced Mr. Trudeau would have remained: if the state was going to force some people to speak two particular languages, when many of the people spoke other languages, how could the state avoid at least recognizing those other languages and the people who spoke them? Once the state intervenes in an everyday matter like language, instead of letting the citizens sort out on their own whatever difficulties they might have, it is soon drawn to intervene again. Hence Mr. Trudeau's declaration of policy quoted above: "A policy of multiculturalism within a bilingual framework....The government will support and encourage the various cultures and ethnic groups that give structure and vitality to our society."

As it happened, that particular intervention fitted conveniently into the longer-range fulfilment of Canada's new role as prototype for tomorrow's federation of the world. As Lester Pearson told the Couchiching Conference in 1968, Canadians should work to create a new kind of internationalism rather than trying to reinforce national independence. If the role were to be fulfilled it was obviously counter-productive to look only to yesterday's sources of immigrants: the net must be cast world-wide until Canada had not merely a policy of polyglotism but the appearance of it as well.

Now you might think that immigration, which plays such a large part in determining the make-up of a country, would be a matter for consultation and at least some sort of agreement with the people who lived there already. But if you lived in Canada during the 1960s you would be wrong on three counts. First, you had a prime minister's office with near-dictatorial power inhabited by a prime minister who wanted to rid Canada of the British tradition; second you had a bevy of mandarins for whom changing regulations without the fuss of going to Parliament was a welcome challenge; and third you had a mass of citizens who were used to trusting their governments to be good and to keep the peace.

Thus when it began to dawn on citizens at large that the rules had been changed, it was too late for them to do anything about it other than to form voluntary associations in the way the Leitches had done for the language business. Once immigrant flows had been changed, once the government had put in train its "support and encouragement of the various ethnic groups" who naturally used the subsidies to browbeat politicians into widening the doors for groups of their particular ethnicities, no political leader, and very, very few elected politicians would dare to be heard or seen opposing the changes.

At the time – the rules were changed on October 1, 1967 – Canadians were predominantly of Euro/British stock (96.8 percent in the 1961 census). The new regulations ensured that the ethnic balance would be changed under the pretext of fairness to all. "An assessment system permits immigration officers to apply the same standards in the same way to potential immigrants from all areas of the world. The regulations formally confirm that Canadian citizens or permanent residents of Canada are entitled to bring their dependents to Canada; the privilege of citizens or permanent residents in applying for more distant relatives to come to Canada is extended to all areas of the world as new classes of relatives become eligible."[4]

In fact the rules discriminated against independent immigrants. Immigrants were now split into three classes: sponsored dependents, nominated (non-dependent) relatives, and independent applicants who were neither sponsored nor nominated.

For sponsored dependents this meant little change: married immigrants from Europe/Britain would expect to bring, and be responsible for, their immediate families.

The second category, nominated (non-dependent) relatives, constituted a change of far-reaching significance. As a former vice-chairman of the Immigration Appeal Board, Charles M. Campbell, told a meeting of the Euro-British Immigration Aid Association in Toronto, May 16, 1989:

> Family Class immigration is favoured by those without an economic base at home and for whom Canada's social support system has special attraction. The process excludes young people whose parents in their middle years are established in their careers at home and are not prepared to emigrate. These are essentially people from the United Kingdom, Europe, the United States, and former British Dominions. They must apply as independents to be selected under restrictive criteria.[5]
>
> In 1982, the Minister limited independent admissions to those taking jobs for which no Canadians were available. Immigration from the United Kingdom dropped from 20,000 to 5,000 annually. It has never recovered. There was no parallel control over family admissions. In 1986 the Minister rescinded that order, increased admissions criteria and imposed a restrictive occupations list. Thousands with skills and talents needed in Canada are still being denied....
>
> In the six years since the entry of the independents was restricted we have admitted a total of 425,000 as refugees, under sponsorship and through the Administrative Review. For none of these was merit a consideration and the advantages of sponsorship continue to be available to them. We have also admitted, for their skills and talents, 120,000 independents for few of whom is sponsorship

available. Their kin must face the restrictive admissions criteria. In the absence of positive action, this assures a continuing uncontrolled flow of immigrants into Canada.

In over three years and dozens of appearances before service clubs and open line radio and television programmes, I have had virtually no negative reaction. This experience and every poll I have seen tells me the people of Canada are strongly opposed to what is happening.

In all this, it was the third category, the independents with skills and aptitudes to make their own way, that was penalized. And while the barriers to independents rose ever higher, the total numbers were unchanged; in other words the proportions of nominated relatives, and later refugees, increased at the expense of the independents.

In 1967, two-thirds of immigrants were independent people whose personal qualities predisposed them to assimilation. The remaining third – family class – consisted of their close relatives. None of today's multitude of settlement services was needed. But since 1980 almost half the immigrants knew neither English nor French when they arrived.[6] By 1988, although family class still made up one third of the total, almost half of the total consisted of the new "assisted relatives" category (24.4 percent) and refugees (22.5 percent) neither of which were subject to the selection criteria that were applied rigidly to independents. Moreover, Canada's immigration offices abroad were required to deal first with family class applicants, second with refugees, and last with the independents who wished to come here to work.

Nor was it any longer true that immigrants strengthened the economy. They used to, but since 1978 the trend had reversed. Independent immigrants still generally contributed to Canada's economic growth, but the family-sponsored and refugee groups that outnumbered them two to one were increasingly less productive.[7]

Canada enjoys an honoured place among nations, and many, many people want to come here. Surely we owe it to them, as well as to ourselves, to preserve the characteristics that make Canada attractive: law abiding, tolerant but not indulgent, hardworking?

This brings us back to "we." It may even be that a majority of Canadians would agree with the sentiment in that last paragraph. But politicians and political leaders are under constant pressure from the government-funded staffs of ethno-cultural councils who serve as Canada's Thought Police. Not only is there no debate in the public press; there is no debate in Parliament either. The only aspect of the topic that is considered safe for discussion is the size of the planned intakes and how they are to be split between the different categories of immigrant. Yet it's patently absurd to admit 250,000 people a year to a country where unemployment ranges from over 10 percent in Toronto to over 30 percent in St. John's.[8]

Let's look at the effect of the changes upon prospective immigrants from Great Britain and Europe – regions that made up 96.8 percent of the source population at the time of the change.

With sponsored dependents there was little change. It was the second category, nominated non-dependent relatives, that changed the whole structure of immigration.

How many British/European immigrants would wish to be followed by sons and daughters aged twenty-one or over, married sons and daughters under twenty-one, brothers, sisters, parents or grandparents under sixty, nephews, nieces, uncles, aunts, and grandchildren?

How many of such non-dependent relatives would wish to leave their families, jobs, friends, homes in Britain or Europe for the uncertainties and unfamiliarities of a new land just because a brother, sister, father- or mother-in-law, uncle, aunt, nephew, niece, or grandparent had gone there? As the economies of Britain and Europe strengthened and prospered, why would they want to leave?

Conversely, how many such non-dependent relatives would understandably welcome the opportunity of exchanging an old life in a Third World country for a new life in Canada? Twenty years after the change, on December 30, 1987, *The Globe and Mail* reported that Harbhajan Singh Pandori, who came to Canada from the Punjab in July 1970, was himself the magnet for, on his estimate, "about sixty to seventy family members" who had joined him in Canada. The report concluded that if friends and neighbours were taken into account, Mr. Pandori's connections stretched to a few hundred immigrants.

This is in no way a criticism of Mr. Pandori, rather it illustrates how Canadian government policy made it possible for him to achieve what he did. That the achievement might have been at the expense of other independent people from Britain or Europe who were just as eager to enter Canada is irrelevant: the regulations were stacked against them. In 1991, for example, an article of mine about immigration in *The London Free Press* brought an appeal for help from a man and his wife, both of them holding doctorates in their fields of science, who had come to Canada from Poland on temporary assignments at the University of Western Ontario. They wished to immigrate to Canada, but were prevented by the regulations. In a letter to then Immigration Minister Barbara McDougall, the wife asked for help, and added: "I would like to ask you very much to do something more: to change the present immigration policy that discriminates against intellectuals coming to Canada – who are not refugees. I am sure it is not only me who would like to offer my best to your country. I'm convinced that it would be good for Canada to accept some foreign scientists, artists and other highly educated people. We would not only bring our knowledge here. We would bring a challenge to those who have been here a long time. We would have to be hardworking and active – simply because it would be the only way to achieve something in a new environment. I do believe it would be good for the country...."

I appealed to Alan Redway MP, not their representative, but a good man (the couple was not of course eligible to vote anywhere), and through his determined efforts on the couple's behalf they were awarded temporary extension of their visas with three days to spare. In February 1992, they and their children became landed immigrants.

In that same period, aid was sought from the (voluntary) Euro-British Immigration Aid Association by many would-be immigrants who had been refused entry to Canada because they were not awarded enough "points" to qualify. Some had been refused many times, yet were still trying.

Typical were the following:

• Wood machine operator/maintenance man, from England,

age 30, married with three children, father and mother and all other relatives in Canada.

- Home improvement specialist, from England, age 28, fluent in English and French, with assets.
- Aircraft engineering supervisor, from England, age 41, 13 years experience, relatives in Canada.
- Petrochemical chief engineer, from Yugoslavia, age 42, married with one child, mother in Canada.
- Craftsman bookbinder, from England, age 38, offered employment, sister in Canada.
- Electrical engineer, from Scotland, age 33, eight years experience in installing X-ray equipment and dialysis machines in hospitals in Scotland, relatives in Canada.
- Commercial photographer, from England, wife of a research assistant, has a daughter born in Vancouver, was successfully employed in Vancouver, extension of work permit refused, family forced to leave Canada.
- Air pilot (single-engine), from Yugoslavia, age 26, fluent in English, pilot certificate in both Yugoslavia and the U.S.
- Artist/teacher/designer, single woman living in the U.S., age 50, fluent in English and French, with assets.
- Film/video technician, from Scotland, extensive experience with BBC television and other programmes as a freelancer, sister in Vancouver.
- Electronics engineer (Ph.D.), from Beijing, studied in Canada for four years, good English, very high qualifications and references.
- Graduate engineer (Ph.D.), from Poland, studied in Canada for five years, fluent English.
- Ph.D. in chemistry, from England, presently working in Ottawa as research associate, living in Canada now over five years, a single mother, work extension refused.
- Specialist decorator, from England, age 33, wife is a nurse's aid, employment available as well as sponsorship by his church, sister in Vancouver.
- Couple, both engineer/economists, from former Czechoslovakia, now residing in the U.S., two children, employment available.

- Welder/equipment repair specialist, from England, age 31, married with two children, employment available, sister, relatives in Canada.

These, the independent people, hitherto mostly British, European, American, or from the old Dominions, who wanted to come on their own initiative, ready and eager to work, were the ones who faced the new barriers. Now, initiative, enterprise, courage, willingness to work were not nearly enough. They must pass tests based on education and training, they must have jobs to come to; above all, they must satisfy immigration officials that they had an acceptable kind of skill, were the right age, knew English or French, had relatives in Canada, and were going somewhere in Canada where the kinds of work they were qualified for were available.

As if this weren't enough, new regulations were introduced in February 1974, "linking the entry of unsponsored [independent] immigrants more closely to the needs of Canadian employers. An immigrant intending to enter the labour force must have a firm job offer from a Canadian employer or an occupation in which there are known to be persistent vacancies in the region of Canada in which he intends to settle."[9]

This imposed a new, higher, barrier. Now, it wasn't enough to face the immigration officials' required tests; immigrants must face the built-in headwinds of the private sector's trade, industrial, and professional associations. How likely was the Steelworkers' Union to admit there were vacancies for steelworkers? Or the International Association of Machinists for aircraft assemblers? Or a provincial medical association for doctors? Or a law society for lawyers? Or a teachers' federation for teachers?

Even though trade unions represented only a third of all tradespeople and a much lower proportion of service workers, the unions' assessments of employment openings were applied across the board. The effect was to close most trade and service vocations to prospective immigrants regardless of qualification or experience or readiness to work; they were simply turned away. For example, on September 14, 1990, the *Toronto Star* reported that by the time the interests of trades unions and professional associations had been satisfied, the list of some 7,700 Canadian job categories shrank to about 120 "available" for immigrants. Of the ten points available under "occupation" in the points system, funeral directors and social workers would get the full ten, aircraft mechanics and electronic equipment repairers would get one, and engineers none.

Yet while the barriers to independents rose ever higher, there was no allowance for this in the total numbers authorized. In other words, as the numbers of sponsored dependents/family class increased, and as the numbers of nominated non-dependent relatives/assisted relatives – and, later, refugees – increased also, they did so at the expense of the numbers of independent prospective immigrants. Moreover, while independent immigrants had to meet tough government criteria, the others were in effect selected by their relatives. In the *Toronto Star*, May 26, 1992, Immigration Minister Bernard Valcourt was quoted as saying, "Last year, we only selected 16 percent of our immigrants. We need a better balance."

The sole requirement of family class was that they be of good health and character (who was to attest to these qualities was not specified). No other government criteria, no points system to pass, just a sponsor's statement promising to provide for their care and maintenance for a period of up to ten years.

Assisted relatives were first assessed on the point system. However, if they couldn't qualify in their own right, they could apply as dependents of a relative who was being sponsored by another relative who was resident in Canada. For sponsoring them, the relative who was himself being sponsored would then get up to fifteen bonus points on his own application, and his pass mark would be reduced from seventy points to fifty-five out of a hundred.

In 1967, the last year before the rules were changed, of 222,876 immigrants, 66.6 percent were independent. The remaining third were "family class" – close relatives of the independent immigrants. In 1968, independents were down to 60.1 percent, family class to 20.8 percent, but the new assisted relative class was 19.1 percent. By 1971, independents were down to 48.5 percent; family class were 27.4 percent, and assisted relatives 24.1 percent.[10]

In his 1982 report to Parliament, Canada's Auditor General Kenneth Dye devoted a full section (section 7) to criticism of immigration procedures: family class loopholes open to abuse (the class which "accounted for approximately 40 percent of the total flow"); lack of control at ports of entry and, after entry, within Canada; selection system circumvented; unlawful tactics used to obtain landed status; increase in "minister's permits" from 9,100 in 1979 to 26,300 in 1981. (A minister's permit is defined as "a written permit issued by the Minister, authorizing a person to come into or remain in Canada if that person, seeking entry, is a member of an inadmissible class, or if already in Canada, has been subject of a report.")

Mr. Dye's report was ignored by Parliament, and by the press. Only one reporter (Vancouver's Jack Webster) sought an interview with him.

In 1982, new restrictions reduced still further the flow of independent immigrants. From Great Britain especially, the number fell from 21,924 in 1981 to 4,456 in 1985. Since 1982, tens of thousands of independent immigrants have been denied entry to Canada, most of them Britons and Europeans.[11]

In 1989 Employment and Immigration Canada issued a pamphlet which included this statement of policy: "The Immigration Act and Regulations are based on such fundamental principles as non-discrimination; family reunion; humanitarian concern for refugees; and the promotion of Canada's social, economic, demographic, and cultural goals."[12]

Let us set this policy against two hypothetical cases. First is that of an experienced electronic equipment repairer in Germany who has no relatives and no arranged employment in Canada, and must get 70 points out of 100 to be considered. (If he had no experience and no arranged employment, he would be barred automatically.) Under specific vocational preparation he might get ten points out of fifteen for a loss of five; for experience, perhaps two out of eight for a loss of six (would have to requalify in Canada); for occupation, one out of ten for a loss of nine. He has no arranged employment so loses ten more, speaks only German and English for a loss of six. Even with six out of ten for personal suitability his total is only sixty points and he is refused entry.

Second is that of a young man somewhere in Asia, which supplied 41 percent of immigrants in 1988 (compared to 21 percent from Europe and 5 percent from Britain). Like his European contemporary, he is unable to qualify in his own right, but he has an uncle who is a Canadian resident and he is admitted as an assisted relative. The uncle himself might be one of an extended family chain of assisted relatives, all in turn tracing sponsorship to a relative who immigrated before the point system was introduced.

The outcome of these two cases might satisfy the principle of family reunion, hardly of non-discrimination. And what social, economic, demographic, and cultural goals are satisfied by Canada's preferring the second applicant to the first?

For the answer to that question we return to the opening paragraph of this chapter, section 27 of the Charter that requires it to "be interpreted in a manner consistent with the preservation and enhancement of the multicultural heritage of Canadians." That statement crops up again in the Immigration Act to explain the apparent discrimination against our German applicant, to wit: "Part I, para 3 (f): to ensure that any person who seeks admission to Canada on either a permanent or temporary basis is subject to standards of admission that do not discriminate in a manner inconsistent with the Canadian Charter of Rights and Freedoms."

In other words, immigration flows must reflect Canada's constitutional requirement that its "multicultural heritage" be enhanced, that is, increased, and how could it be increased unless the components of the world's multitudinous cultures were given preference over the few (chiefly European and British) cultures that predominated before? In fact, the Constitution goes further. Section 15 (2), which provides for affirmative action programmes, states that the equality and non-discrimination sub-section that precedes it "does not preclude any law, programme or activity that has as its object the amelioration of conditions of disadvantaged individuals or groups including those that are disadvantaged because of race, national or ethnic origin, colour, religion, sex, age or mental or physical disability." The laws, programmes, or activities of Canada's immigration practices which have ameliorated the conditions of Canadians who might otherwise have been separated from their extended families are clearly constitutional –

under a constitution, let us remind ourselves, that was changed without our prior consent or subsequent approval.

The present system, biased as it is against independent immigrants from whatever source, is self-fulfilling, witness these passages from the 1983 *Annual Report to Parliament on Immigration Levels*:

> Family class immigration planning is responsive to the number of applications the government expects to receive abroad from eligible family members with sponsors in Canada. The number of these applications has been relatively stable in the past few years; there were 45,540 family class landings in 1978 [total immigration was 86,313]; 46,763 in 1979 [total was 112,096]; 51,039 in 1980 [143,117]; and 51,019 in 1981 [128,618].
>
> Effective October 16, 1981, visitors from India were required to obtain visas abroad before coming to Canada. The requirement was introduced to prevent persons from India coming to Canada solely for the purpose of making a claim to Convention refugee status, and to ensure that persons who do not meet visa requirements would be spared the time and expense of a futile journey from India to Canada.
>
> The staff of the Canadian High Commission in New Delhi has been increased by six visa officers from Canada and twelve locally engaged support staff, bringing the total immigration staff at the mission to thirteen Canadian officers and thirty-four support staff. The facility in New Delhi is now the largest of Canada's immigration posts abroad. To facilitate the processing of applications by persons outside New Delhi, the High Commission has placed advertisements in Indian newspapers explaining how visitor visa applications may be obtained.

Meanwhile, rigid application of the points system in Britain and Europe, and the resulting decline in independent immigrants, led to the closing of immigration offices there. In the British Isles, for example, the only immigration office was in London, where 80 percent of applicants were being rejected.

The quoted passages are a snapshot of how the policy was self-fulfilling: selection "criteria" favoured family class and assisted relatives. By funding "ethnic" associations and allotting bonus points to sponsoring relatives, the government "supported and encouraged" family reunification. In the government's India example, as Canada's Indian community grew, and was fed by the government's "multicultural" grants (for example, $131,000 in 1984 to the National Association of Canadians of Origins in India), so also grew the demands, from Canadians of origins in India, to expand intakes from India, a pattern other groups were quick to follow. (Other examples from the same year were: $56,635 to the Multicultural Society of Kelowna; $39,000 to the Council of India Societies of Edmonton; $42,540 to the Calgary Vietnamese Canadian Association; $60,000 to the Chinese Benevolent Association; and $33,109 to l'Association des médecins haitiens a l'étranger.) [13]

Finally, the assumption of Canada's being a multicultural country reinforced the pressure to concentrate immigration efforts toward non-traditional sources. Immigration Minister Lloyd Axworthy expressed the Liberal Party's view in the House of Commons, May 24, 1980, when he said: "We are not trying to maintain the old stereotypes of what is a Canadian."

What, no one was brave enough to ask at the time, were they trying to maintain? Certainly not the old stereotype that so impressed me before, during and since the Second World War.

Here is a curious thing. Mr. Trudeau's Charter guarantees among other things "freedom of thought, belief, opinion and expression, including freedom of the press and other media of communication...subject only to such reasonable limits prescribed by law as can be demonstrably justified in a free and democratic society."

Thus am I free to express my opinion about successive Canadian governments' immigration policies. Or am I? Suppose those reasonable limits stop at my criticism of the policies because one of the state's commissions or tribunals invokes the Charter to justify an accusation that such criticism is "racist" and therefore discriminatory, and thus offends section 15 (1)? Or suppose a judge who is entitled under the new dispensation to interpret the supreme law of Canada in a way that seems reasonable to him or her decides that my criticism of immigration policies constitutes a breach of section 15 (1) in that I am advocating "discrimination based on race, national or ethnic origin, colour, religion, sex, age or mental or physical disability." Would it matter that I wasn't advocating discrimination, but the reverse, namely to stop the discrimination? Probably not. For Catch 22 turns up, as I mentioned just now, in the next section 15 (2), where it's OK for government to "ameliorate" the conditions of people who might be disadvantaged for the reasons stated in 15 (1), and therefore if I were shown to oppose that other kind of discrimination I'd be in trouble again.

Once again, I declare my bias. It is for freedom of the individual to do or say anything that is not forbidden by the law; and against the use of arbitrary power to prevent that freedom's exercise.

Now let us leave the formal law for the moment and see what happens in the court of "public opinion" as interpreted by Canada's media. In that court I would be stigmatized as a racist or worse, for it is common knowledge that except in the privacy of one's home, and among very close friends, immigration to Canada is a forbidden topic. Anyone who dares to mention it in public, let alone criticize present policy, is immediately dubbed racist by the government-funded staffs of ethno-cultural councils who serve as Canada's Thought Police. Not only is there no debate in the public press; there is no debate in Parliament either. The only aspect of the topic that is considered safe for discussion is the size of the planned intakes and how they are to be split between the different categories of immigrant.

Government funding enables ethnic-based pressure groups to maintain full-time staffs who then demand special treatment for intending immigrants from the groups' countries of origin. Vote-hungry politicians court these same "multicultural" groups, and a self-sustaining, government-funded multicult industry acts as a barrier against the immigrants' assimilation into the majority Canadian culture.

This brings us back to Lloyd Axworthy and the question of what he and the Liberal Party, as well as their Progressive Conservative successors, were trying to maintain. From the post-1980 record, it appears that they were trying with considerable success to maintain the results I've described as the outcome of the 1967 policy change, albeit at a slightly slower rate.

In the Immigration Department's 1991–1995 Immigration Plan, the planned intakes remained at 250,000 annually, but there was some juggling among the different categories. Although by 1995 Family Class would decline by six percent from 100,000 (40 percent) to 85,000 (34 percent), the associated Assisted Relatives would rise from 19,500 (7.8 percent) to 30,500 (12.2 percent), in total a negligible drop in this key category from 119,500 to 115,500 (from 47.8 percent to 46.2 percent).

Privately sponsored refugees would decline from 20,000 (8 percent) to 15,000 (6 percent); and business immigrants plus their spouses and other accompanying dependents from 28,000 (11.2 percent) to 19,500 (7.8 percent). Retirees would cease to be admitted after 1992. At the same time, government assisted refugees would be unchanged at 13,000 (5.2 percent), and refugees landed in Canada after January 1, 1989, would be unchanged at 25,000 (10 percent).

Increases were authorized in the independent category, which together with spouses and other accompanying relatives, would rise from 41,500 (16.6 percent) to 61,000 (24.4 percent), but the points system would still apply to the independents. That is to say, an eighteen-year-old youth who had the desire and courage to make his own way in Canada, but who had neither a resident relative, nor job experience nor arranged employment, would be barred automatically on either of those two latter counts. But if he were the spouse or fiancé of a Canadian resident he would be admitted provided he met "health, security and criminality requirements." If he were the brother of a Canadian resident, although he would have to meet those requirements and would also have to qualify through the points system, having "a close relative in Canada" would entitle him to additional points. In short, the system was still skewed toward large extended families and against independent individuals. The government-subsidized ethno-cultural associations were still in place to perpetuate the flows from the countries their members had left.

Lest readers equate what I am saying with a conservative view of events, let me reassure them by citing these extracts from

Michael Valpy's January 13, 1995, column in *The Globe and Mail*. In it, he quoted with approval from an article, "The Immigration Reform That Wasn't," that had appeared in the latest issue of *Canada Watch*, the publication of York University's Robarts Centre for Canadian Studies and its Centre for Public Law and Public Policy. The author, James Hathaway, is one of Canada's most respected immigration experts, an associate professor of Osgoode Hall Law School, and director of York University's Refugee Law Research. Valpy wrote that among Professor Hathaway's criticisms are that Minister of Immigration Sergio Marchi presented no clear vision of why Canada admits so many family members, "a mammoth proportion of our immigration quota," or why their definition is so broad; why in fact Canada admits six times more family immigrants than refugees; why it hasn't favoured independent immigrants "at a time when carefully targeted independent immigrants could contribute to the economic recovery." To this Hathaway supplies an answer: that it lies in politics. As Valpy interprets it: "Recent arrivals to Canada are more cohesive in their political behaviour than more established residents. Voters from non-dominant cultures play a pivotal role in 30 federal ridings. Refugees and economic migrants have nothing close to the political clout of voters who wish to bring their families to Canada."

Professor Hathaway also stated that unless overall quotas are increased, the pressure to accept relatives makes balanced immigration planning "almost impossible." He would narrow the definition of family to spouses and dependent children, in other words (though he did not say this) to where the policy stood before the revolution.

In the January 1995 issue of *Chronicles*, London freelance writer Derrick Turner, an Irishman by birth but self-styled as always having been conscious of "some affinity for Britain, and particularly England" and who always felt at home there, described his experience since he went to live in London in 1988 and "roamed far and wide" until he came to know the city "far better than Dublin, and far better than most Londoners."

He was startled to find not only that "large chunks" of London were "not English"; they weren't even *British*, and that the effect of importing huge numbers of people from dissimilar backgrounds, countries and races, speaking different languages and practicing different religions was to pose "a real danger of British culture and civilization vanishing forever." However extreme this conclusion may sound, it needs only to reflect on some of the examples he quotes – such as when thousands of Muslims gathered in Parliament Square with placards proclaiming "Islam: Today Our Religion, Tomorrow Your Religion" to demand the death of Salman Rushdie, and such as the fact that soon after the turn of the century white Britons will be an ethnic minority in four London boroughs – to realize the significance of successive Canadian governments' immigration policies designed to fulfill the constitutionally imposed requirements of "multiculturalism."

In the *Toronto Star* of September 27, 1993, columnist Frank Jones reported that open street fighting had broken out in London's East End after a member of the British National Party was elected to the local council. "'We're going to take our country back,' Beackon told his white supporters in a predominantly Asian and black area."

Jones continued: "Shocking, you say. Stick around. It won't be long, I predict, before you'll see the same kind of thing happening right here in Toronto....Beackon was elected in London largely because of white resentment that much of the public housing is now occupied by Asians and blacks."

Noting that his job took him all over the city and to every sort of home, Jones wrote, "It's taboo to draw attention to it, but many public housing developments now have the appearance of Third World villages. Today 25 percent of the population in this region is non-white; by 2001 that figure is expected to reach 45 per cent."

Jones's estimate is supported by Statistics Canada figures released in December 1992 and reported in *The Globe and Mail* on December 9 by its social trends reporter, Alanna Mitchell. The figures showed that whereas in 1961, 90 percent of immigrants to Canada came from European countries, between 1981 and 1991 the number from Europe had fallen to 25 percent. In that same period, 1981–91, almost half of all immigrants were born in Asia, and 38 percent of Toronto's population was immigrant, that is, people not born in Canada but granted the right to live here permanently.

Mitchell quoted Ellen Gee, a sociologist at Simon Fraser University. Ms. Gee said that immigration patterns had changed so rapidly as to result in "a recipe for social unease. 'Survey after survey shows that people are negative about immigrants. I'm very pessimistic. Basically, what we're dealing with...is racism.'"

Three out of five immigrants to Canada go to its three largest cities: Toronto, Montreal, and Vancouver. In 1993, Toronto took 71,956 immigrants, of whom 14,220 were from Hong Kong, about 8,000 from the Caribbean, and large numbers from India and the Philippines. More than half the immigrants to Ontario spoke neither English nor French. Since Toronto is Canada's largest city, comparable in that respect to London's position in the United Kingdom, it is worth translating the comparison into numbers. According to figures Derrick Turner took from the 1991 British census, the non-European settlement is concentrated in certain boroughs: 40–50 percent of the population in the boroughs of Brent and Newham, 30–40 percent in Tower Hamlets, Lewisham, Ealing, and Hackney, then smaller but still substantial numbers in all other London boroughs, except those on the borders of Kent and Essex.

From Canada's 1991 census we find that in the Greater Toronto Area 144,625 persons did not have a working knowledge of English, an increase of 37.6 percent since 1986. Persons of British origin numbered 857,655, or 20.2 percent of the population, a decline of 21.9 percent since 1986. For the first time, Canadian origin was included as a category, and 306,720 persons declared accordingly, 7.2 percent of the total. Those of Italian origin declined from 8 percent (298,020) in 1986 to 7.5 percent (318,310) in 1991; Jewish from 2.9 percent (109,325) to 2.7 percent (115,300); while Portuguese increased slightly from 2.6 percent (98,550) to 2.9 percent (124,890).

Persons with Chinese ethnic origin grew from 128,095 in 1986 (3.4 percent of the total) to 234,440 (5.5 percent) in 1991, an increase of 83 percent. Those of East Indian ancestry were not recorded in 1986; they numbered 144,335 (3.4 percent) in 1991. Persons with Black ethnic origin grew from 92,600 (2.5 percent) in 1986 to 128,040 (3 percent) in 1991.

In 1991, the Greater Toronto Area had a population of

4,260,000 distributed among five regional municipalities: Metro Toronto, Durham, Peel, York, and Halton. Metro Toronto had the largest population (2,290,000) and in 1993 its planning department projected an increase from a 1986 figure of 21 percent visible minorities to 32 percent by 2001. Peel, which was next in size (740,000), had 24.8 percent visible minorities by 1991, while three years later the region's planning department projected population growth to one million by 2001 of which one-third would consist of visible minorities.[14]

Now it may be that Canadians' celebrated tolerance will enable those of them who live in the major cities to absorb the large numbers of people whose origins, languages, and cultures are not merely different from, but often at odds with, the Canadian mainstream. Personal impressions from observing the children of neighbours where we live in Metro Toronto as well as a grandson's friends and classmates at a York Region high school, many of them of Chinese or Indian parentage, suggest that this is so: the second generation grows up Canadian. Another impression, gained some years ago, supports it from another angle: a mason from Jamaica maintained that although "the British left Jamaica too soon," the chief reason he chose to come to Canada was its British heritage and common law tradition (he was an amateur of the law). That sentiment, and the reason behind it, may very well extend to many immigrants who, however patently they belong to a visible minority may belong also to the invisible majority that constitutes heritage in the British Commonwealth.

This is not a book about immigration, nor even about multiculturalism, but rather about the misuse of arbitrary power to impose the views of small groups of people upon their fellows. If the dramatic changes in immigration patterns that were imposed on Canadians without seeking either their prior consent or subsequent approval have led to unfortunate results among the people of our large cities, I think it is not nearly enough, in fact it is probably counterproductive, to establish commissions and tribunals to "combat racism," install hiring quotas and so on. Rather might we let people get used to one another at their own speed in the Canadian way, recognize that the changes have been too rapid for comfort (per capita, Canada takes in 2.5 times as many immigrants as the United States), and simply call a halt for two or three years. Go on an immigration diet and soothe the national digestion.[15]

Any discussion of multiculturalism cannot fail to be contentious, and not only because views of any kind will be attacked by one or other of the government-subsidized full-time staffs of ethno-cultural groups who leap upon such opportunities to justify their existences – and subsidies. Culture is very much a matter of the heart; as the dictionary has it: The training, development, and refinement of mind, morals, or taste.

On a visit to Montreal after the massive anglo exodus that followed the passage of the French-only language laws (Bill 22 and its successor Bill 101), I caught on the evening news an interview with a French-speaking Canadian who was about to leave the city for a job in Alberta. When he was asked about missing his language and his culture, he replied: "Language is an affair of the stomach. We speak in order to eat. But culture [placing his hand on his heart] is an affair of the heart. I take my culture with me."

Twenty years later, on June 27, 1994, Kirk Makin of *The Globe and Mail* wrote a long and percipient analysis of multiculturalism policy, and one of the parts that struck me was the statement by Peter Samaras, a Toronto furrier, who was a board member of the city's Greek association, "yet loathed the psychological effects of multiculturalism. 'I left Greece to come here as a sixteen-year-old boy,' he said. 'I *left* it, you know? I still have family in Greece, but I came to live here and do the best I can for this country. I don't believe in multiculturalism; they want to keep me a Greek. Somebody has to put their feet down and say: enough.'"

Who that somebody might be is very much up in the air, in fact in the stratosphere inhabited by the members of Canada's New Class.

· SIX ·

The political influence of Canada's New Class — known also as the Court Party for its attachment to legislated rights — was reflected in the annual samplings of nation-wide opinion by *Maclean's* magazine. In January 1991, for example, the sampling showed that 60 percent of respondents in English Canada would like to see a federal system that gave all provinces more independence from Ottawa. Twenty-four percent wanted no change to the existing system, while 10 percent wanted to give Ottawa much more power. At first glance, that only 10 percent favoured a much stronger central government was a surprisingly small percentage. Any regular scanner of Canada's print and electronic media could not have escaped the impression that such an opinion was widely held. What the poll did was to show the difference between the perception and the reality. The 10 percent included the opinion-makers whose views were heard and reheard, published and republished throughout the land. The 60 percent who favoured devolution were members of a majority whose views were unheard and unpublished, and for whom no one spoke save the compilers of opinion polls.

The New Class whose opinions dominate Canada's media is composed of people who share a certain view both of themselves and of the society they live in. It is drawn from the ranks of political clergy, union leaders, the government-paid staffs of women's groups and francophone and ethnic associations, university professors, senior civil servants, human rights and language commissioners, senior businesspeople, print and electronic journalists, writers and actors and playwrights. The system of top-down government imposed on the country through Pierre Trudeau's written Charter is so fundamental to the creation and maintenance of a New Class that its spokesmen assume it is best not only for them but for everyone. It enables them to use political power to shape society in their image. The threat they pose to society is not so much that they mean well as that not only their good intentions but also the eventual outcomes are financed at everyone else's expense. Their attitudes are self-styled by such words as compassionate, caring, tolerant, humane, charitable, and above all progressive — adjectives that by inference apply also to the opinion-makers themselves. They see society as an abstraction which it is their responsibility, using the coercive power of the State, to stamp with their image. That is the sort of people they are, they know what is best for society as a collection of other people, and consequently what they decide must be for the best. They have become so addicted to the drug of the state as cure-all that their opponents' view (that over-government is a leading cause of society's ills) is not merely laughable, it is characteristic of people who are pitiless, uncaring, intolerant, inhumane, uncharitable, and reactionary. Thus opinion-makers regard themselves as occupying the moral high ground from which they can stigmatize opponents as bigots, racists, and rednecks who think only of themselves and who would drag society backwards into what the New Class regards as the dog-eat-dog jungle of unrestricted private enterprise.

It is the New Class's influence that has led directly to over-blown governments and a crippling national debt. Yet its members are a minority. Not surprisingly, therefore, the *Maclean's*/Decima poll also found that 60 percent of respondents wanted a more direct say in government, 55 percent wanted the power to recall MPs, 52 percent wanted to tell politicians how taxes should be spent, 77 percent wanted balanced budgets, 77 percent wanted public consultation before governments made major decisions, and 89 percent were opposed to MPs voting the party line: they should vote either according to conscience or to the expressed views of constituents. In short, the majority of Canadians whose voices had been drowned out by those of Canada's New Class wanted their voices not merely to be heard, but also to be acted upon. They wanted referendums on major issues of policy that had until then been decided without consulting them, such as radically changed immigration, official bilingualism, official multiculturalism, public overspending, and changing the Constitution.

Curiously, many successful entrepreneurs and businesspeople who head corporations, and who might be expected to stand up for freedom, are too often recruited into the New Class as well. Not only is it fashionable for them to be associated with the opinion-makers, they are also instrumental in perpetuating the opinions; corporations and successful entrepreneurs vie with one another in their financial support both of the universities whose faculties mold the opinion-makers, and of the political parties that turn the opinions into law.

Politicians and party leaders alike are trapped in what is not so much a system, although that has a lot to do with it, as an atmosphere. It is fashionable to pretend that Canada's culture should be buried in multiculturalism; that it would be immoral for Canada to favour migrants from its traditional sources; that labour unions are democracies in miniature and that the regular occurrence of violence during strikes is a freak of nature, like the weather; that French Canadians have been wronged from the start and that the rest of the country can never do too much in expiation of its guilt; above all that the people who subscribe to these fashionable pretensions are people in the know, and their view must prevail. In the end, their view can prevail only through co-opting the coercive power of the state, and this is why the politicians are in a box. They are the targets of all the groups that live, breathe, and exude the fashionable atmosphere. Indeed, the Left's capture of Canada's means of communication is so successful, and has been engineered through so many years, as to make the task of presenting another view of society not merely formidable but apparently hopeless. The Left commands the government, which commands the people. In all but name, Canada is a one-party elective dictatorship. Canada's permanent government draws up the rules and enforces them with the power of the State.

All this, you might think, is fine and large, but Canada is still a democracy, and a parliamentary one at that. So what if the New Class has so much influence; don't we need the best and brightest at the top? Didn't Edmund Burke tell the electors of Bristol that when they had chosen him, he was not a member of Bristol, but he was a member of *parliament?* But he also said that "To provide for us in our necessities is not in the power of government. It would be vain presumption in statesmen to think they can do it. The people maintain them, and not they the people. It is in the power of government to prevent much evil; it can do very little positive good in this, or perhaps in anything else."[1]

When Ernest Manning joked about grocery care, this surely was his point. Thirty years later we see the result of statesmen trying to provide for us in our necessities and providing us only with interest bills on the money they borrowed in the attempt.

The question remains: who is to govern? In retrospect we can see the folly of policies, we may even think the policy-makers were foolish, but we can see also the folly of the grand solutions that led them astray. If we the governed wish to be governed by consent, how are we to express it?

In these 1990s there is a flurry for referendums, and it is no doubt a natural reaction to thirty years of government by fiat, using the semblance of democracy to impose arbitrary measures, that people should want a means not only to stop the same thing happening again but also to reverse some of the things that were imposed on them in the past.

Pierre Trudeau's grand solution to Quebec's nationalism was clearly a failure, and there can be little doubt that had his idea been put to the people beforehand in a national referendum, it would have been voted down by a majority. But that doesn't necessarily mean that referendums on major issues like official bilingualism would always work to the general benefit. In that particular instance the majority that voted "No" would likely be composed of mother tongue anglos and "other" residents of the eight English-speaking provinces who lived and worked in English and saw no point in establishing bilingual districts for the tiny percentages of fellow Ontarians or Manitobans who were also living and working in English alongside them. The decline of francophone populations in Saskatchewan noted in chapter 4 despite decades of government-funded artificial respiration suggests that they would have been right. A simple Yes/No vote would have left unresolved the basic issue of French-Canadian nationalism, while the "No" result might have exacerbated French-Canadian feelings, yet that would still have been better than what was done without even asking the question – and exacerbating the feelings of the majority that opposed the policy. A (probably commanding) majority would have spoken and the French language would still be protected by the Constitution.

In short, the referendum would have confirmed the wisdom of the BNA Act's linguistic provisions, and we come back to who is in charge. It is at least arguable that if he had chosen to, a prime minister of Pierre Trudeau's capacities could have "sold" the BNA Act's provisions to his francophone constituents and put up with the ranting of opponents rather than risk turning the country upside down. But he was prevented from so choosing by his trait of consistency, which insulated him from any suspicion that his long-held opinion might be wrong.

The bilingual business is in fact a frightening example of Utopians at work in circumstances – a majority in the House of Commons and a passionate, bilingual ideologue in the prime minister's office – that enabled them to enforce their ideas on a whole country.

Only a man who at the time of his accession to the leadership of the Liberal Party was ignorant of Canada west of Ottawa could have supposed that the francophone presence outside Quebec could be so strengthened by government measures that the provincial premiers in English provinces would speak for francophones as forcefully and effectively as the premier of Quebec. Yet this was Pierre Trudeau's cure for French-Canadian nationalism: once French-language rights were constitutionally entrenched the French-Canadian nation would stretch from coast to coast.

It was of a piece with his approach to government as described by a senior mandarin at the end of the 1970s: "A model that belonged in a university, not in the real world. Like so many of the ideas that the Trudeauites conceived, it was completely rational but deeply impractical. It was based on the belief that you could construct a system and then force not only people but events to fit themselves into it."[2]

It comes back to the power of government, how it is to be exercised and who is to be entrusted with exercising it. George Washington warned us that "Government is not reason; it is not eloquence; it is force. Like fire, it is a dangerous servant and a fearful master."

It is also confused with the state. Government's legitimate role in a free society is to protect the citizens and their property from encroachment and to require the observance of contracts. Once a government steps outside that role, the power it exercises becomes political power. It is political power, funded from everyone's taxes, that the hosts of advocacy groups manipulate to further their private causes. Whereas governmental power is used legitimately to protect us and our property from acts by other citizens to encroach upon it or to break contracts, political power is used to force citizens who are not in breach of the law to do things they don't want to do.

Frédéric Bastiat wrote that "The law can be an instrument of equalization only as it takes from some persons and gives to other persons. When the law does this, it is an instrument of plunder."[3]

In short, government is the agency designed to serve the ends of justice by securing the citizen's rights to life, liberty, and property that are inherent in the common law. But when the law is perverted into an instrument of plunder, the agency that perverts it is the state.[4]

In the story of Pierre Trudeau's political life Canadians have a citizens' guide for what to avoid. They went through the fire to satisfy one man's "overweening pride," in Christina McCall-Newman's phrase.

Readers who remember the annual television "interviews" between Prime Minister Trudeau and CTV's Bruce Phillips will remember also the former's virtuosity. The rule was: Never answer a question; always use it as the peg on which to turn things around to your advantage and puff yourself up.

The master of television and progenitor of the Canadian state's massive growth was himself a child of the media he affected to despise, and in particular of the state's broadcasting agencies.

In his book *Trudeau Revealed*, David Somerville quoted Robert Rumilly (*The Tactics of the Leftists Unmasked*, 1957) on Radio Canada in the late 1950s and early 1960s: "The name of Pierre Elliott Trudeau was projected, acclaimed, repeated hundreds of times to hundreds of thousands of listeners. It's thus that Pierre Elliott Trudeau can pass for an important personage today. His initiatives and interventions carry some weight. All of it in the service of socialist ideas. Hundreds of young people much more gifted than Pierre Elliott Trudeau didn't have the same chance because they weren't on the left."[5]

Yet in 1968 when he assumed power he was portrayed by a captivated media (Peter Newman described him as "an agent of ferment, a critic of Canadian society, questioning its collected conventional wisdom") as a run-of-the-mill Liberal, when he made his commitment to socialism perfectly clear in essays published the same year.

Three decades later, when his carefully staged *Memoirs* were filmed for posterity and then made into a book, the film's producer, Brian McKenna, made no bones about the purpose. "'I think the judgment of history is extremely important to a leader,' he says. 'It's important that it be as favourable as possible.'"[6]

Brian McKenna and his brother Terence, who served as writer and narrator, were described by historian Desmond Morton as "An articulate, mediawise duo with opinions well in the mainstream of the CBC-NFB elite" after they had produced for CBC-NFB a three-part series about Canada's role in the Second World War entitled *The Valour and the Horror*. First aired in January 1992, the second episode, "Death by Moonlight: Bomber Command," was so filled with "dramatizations, inferences, innuendos, depictions, and distortions that are not true" that it became the subject of a lawsuit for defamation against the CBC and others by the surviving aircrews of Bomber Command. The CBC's Ombudsman, William Morgan, whose sixty-page report was cut by CBC's management to thirteen pages before release in order to reduce criticism, found the series "flawed as it stands and fails to measure up to CBC's demanding policies and standards." In their Statement of Claim, the aircrews pleaded that the filmmakers "set about to effect a revision of history so as to conform the facts thereof to their political, or pacifist, or anti-military opinions. In particular, they intended their 'commercial' version to be distributed to educational institutions and primary and secondary school educators to be used as teaching aids for successive generations of Canadian children."[7]

In his review of *Memoirs*, Professor Morton wrote: "As producers, the McKenna brothers (director Brian and scriptwriter Terence) have lent their skill and a deceitful air of documentary authenticity to a series that is about as objective as their earlier television triumph, *The Valour and the Horror*."[8]

In our old age, many of us hanker for the immortality of print.

Vanity presses seek our business and we treat ourselves to what *The New Yorker* once called "infatuation with sound of own words." The camcorder indulges us with the promise of longevity beyond the grave. These pursuits may even contribute in their small and various ways to the durability of families. We may hope to present a favourable view of ourselves, but the posterity we present it to is local and intimate, like the heredity we recognize in the life that is ending. Players on a small stage, we have few pretensions.

Not so for the players on larger stages. Self-regarded as makers of history, it is inexpugnable that their roles were historic. What they said and did must be accorded the importance that springs from their conviction of how important it was, and they were.

Napoleon dictated a long series of apologias to his companions in exile that were designed to create a Napoleonic legend. The first and most influential was the *Mémorial de Sainte Hélène*, which became a best-seller as soon as it appeared in 1823 and went on selling throughout the century. "'I have saved the revolution as it lay dying. I have cleansed it of its crimes and have held it up to the people, shining with glory,' he boasted on St. Helena. 'I have given France and Europe new ideas which will never be forgotten.'...the legend was widely accepted in France where the working class and petit-bourgeoisie looked back with nostalgia to the Empire's comparative material plenty....."[9]

Trudeau showed a remarkable talent for backing into the limelight, and there is no doubt that he coveted the political power he revelled in exercising. But although one author (Philip Resnick) decribed his hijacking of the BNA Act as "Constitutional Bonapartism" he had no military aspirations; his conquests were at the conference table and the polling booth.

That those conquests were in pursuit of political ideas at variance with the Canadian tradition was as much an accident of the times when he achieved them as it was of the voting patterns he was able to profit from. Had he been defeated in 1972 – and it was a close-run thing – Canada would have been spared the festering sores from his National Energy Programme, a national debt of crippling proportions, and a radically changed constitution that substitutes entitlements for responsibilities.

It is entirely consistent with the consistency that governed both his writings and the politics he imposed on us that he was unable to discern their inherent contradictions. He didn't see the contradictions when he was young, his pride stopped him from even considering he might be wrong as he grew older, and as late as 1993, when he was seventy-four, he clung in his *Memoirs* to the same conceits.

A student of the law, he confused law which should serve the ends of justice with the state which misuses the law as an instrument of plunder. As Bastiat warned, the law can be an instrument of equalization only as it takes from some persons and gives to other persons. Yet for Trudeau "equality" was a "value" to be entrenched in his charter. As we saw in chapter 5, equality rights are laid down in sections 15 (1) and (2), and they are contradictory. First, subsection 15 (1) declares that "every individual...has the right to the equal protection and equal benefit of the law without discrimination and, in particular, without discrimination based on race" etc., which means that since the law is to "benefit" individuals equally it must be an instrument of equalization, so that the law gives to some what it has first taken from others. (Equalization between individuals and regions is entrenched in part III.) Second, subsection 15 (2) declares that the previous subsection "does not preclude any law, program or activity that has as its object the amelioration of conditions of disadvantaged individuals or groups including those that are disadvantaged because of race" etc., which means that it's OK for the law to discriminate.

As long ago as 1958 Trudeau was writing what he repeated in his memoirs as "my long-held view" that the law must permit the individual to fulfil himself to the utmost. The individual had certain "basic rights that cannot be taken away by any government." That was why he committed Canadians to a rigid, written charter that would "define a system of values such as liberty, equality, and the rights of association that Canadians from coast to coast could share."

He wanted to define rights that Canadians had enjoyed inherently through their British heritage for centuries and he was blind to the implication: that to define is to limit, and to apply the modifier "reasonable" to those limits was to deliver the hapless citizen into the hands of government-appointed judges who had not only been made the ultimate authority transcending Parliament but were also as susceptible to differing shades of political opinion as anyone else.

His confusion over "equality" might be traced to 1789 and the revolutionary idea that the established order must be destroyed so that a new one could be founded on a rational basis. ("We embarked upon an exercise to change the constitution fundamentally.") The law must be positive – doing things for people who could be made equal in their material lives by the intercessions of government – rather than negative as it had been before, when it merely used its authorized penalties to discourage people from indulging their passions in ways that would harm other people. It was the difference between the belief that man was perfectible (by the means laid down by enlightened guardians), and the belief that because perfection was not of this world the best that could be done was to mitigate the harmful effects of man's imperfection.

The key to Trudeau's contradiction is his use of the word "permit." When he was thirty-nine, he wrote that state control was needed to maximize the liberty and welfare of all, and to permit everyone to realize himself fully. When he was seventy-four, "the subject of law must be the individual human being; the law must permit the individual to fulfil himself or herself to the utmost."[10]

For Trudeau, the law was there, a supernimbus overhanging the whole of Canada. Beneath it the citizens stumbled about in their varying degrees of ignorance searching, searching for a ray that would light their way towards doing something they would secretly like to do if only the law would permit them to attempt it.

In this is exposed the unbridgeable divide between what J.P. Nowlan called "all the rights in the world except those that say, 'Stop at a stop sign, do not drive too fast, do not drink too much and do not kill somebody'" and the civil code wherein "one does not have any right to do anything unless one can point to it in some constitution, some bill of rights or some charter."

It is the divide between a self-regulating society wherein the citizens take personal responsibility for their actions – to break or abide by the law which everyone understands – and a regulated society wherein although no one is sure what judges will rule about laws the citizens don't understand, all the citizens are led to think it worth trying to gain personal advantage from what the laws seem to offer them, and at their neighbours' expense.

To add two more of Alain Peyrefitte's sentences to the one quoted previously: "Excessive governmental responsibility encourages lack of responsibility in the citizen. From this excess and this absence, in fact, have arisen the revolutions and rebellions with which France's history is so replete. Centralization perpetuates the crises it was created to dispel."[11]

Responding to crises "by instituting or expanding central agencies" (Campbell), "constructing a system and then forcing not only people but events to fit themselves into it" (McCall-Newman) – centralization was Trudeau's guide to government. In one man who was granted the near-dictatorial power of a Canadian prime minister with a majority in the House of Commons, Canadians experienced not only the results of that man's confused thinking on the fundamental matter of individual freedom, but also of his putting into practice the incompatibility of his thinking with the federalism that Canada was founded upon.

When I wrote in the foreword that his dominant influence upon events has been tragic for Canada I used the adjective in its sense of being an intensely sad course of events, not fatal, because this great country will recover from them in time, but sad because they were caused by a man who despite his Utopian urges toward a federation of the world was always a patriotic, even a great, Canadian: complex, as are we all, but also confused, as no doubt are we all a good deal of the time, yet bedevilled by an "overweening pride" that most of us manage to stifle after we leave the schoolyard.

Perhaps he was too long in the schoolyard. The immaturities that surfaced in his pirouetting behind the Queen, in his dressing up in stagey clothes, in his embarking upon a first marriage at the age of fifty-one to a woman of twenty-two – these were hardly the marks of a grown man.

Yet he had all that power.

We return to Gibbon: "Of all our passions and appetites, the love of power is of the most imperious and unsociable nature, since the pride of one man requires the submission of the multitude." The Canadian multitude submitted to the pride of Pierre Elliott Trudeau for sixteen years and only now, in this second decade since he quit rather than face the electorate, only now is the country starting to come together; not as it was before he damaged it, but with a vision of its future that is clearer for its having weathered the damage.

Others better qualified than I have written their prescriptions for repairing the damage. Citizen-initiated referendums on major policy issues such as language, culture, immigration, taxes, and debt; abolishing all government funding to advocacy groups; adopting many of Switzerland's proven measures for a durable and solvent democracy – these are the nuts and bolts of sensible reform.

But underpinning them must be the rock of a Constitution that embodies the feelings and instincts of Canadians. Not the weak and unprepossessing base of a mini-United Nations that Professor Rocher ridiculed, but the solid one that is rooted in the British North America Act and the English common law that informs it.

If the hard fact of governmental insolvency persuades us that it is not, after all, in the power of government to provide for us in our necessities, we are lucky to have made the discovery before the damage became irreparable. But we are in another danger: that of failing to understand what went wrong so that our sons and daughters can guard against going wrong again.

It is unfortunate that no one seems to have thought of impeaching Pierre Trudeau when he was in office. Not for anything in his personal life or indeed his personal behaviour as prime minister, but for his political mishandling of the country's finances and his overturning, by fraudulent means, of the Constitution.

Only one American president (Andrew Johnson) has been impeached, and the act of impeachment is so rare an event in the politics of the industrialized world that it has come to be associated with only two names: Warren Hastings, who was the first Governor-General of India, and the United States' thirty-seventh president, Richard Nixon. Hastings was the luckless inheritor of corrupt methods practised by Indian princes. Historian Paul Johnson writes that "Administration by bribery was no longer acceptable in England; it could not be practised elsewhere. Hastings was not a scoundrel: he was an anachronism."[12]

Richard Nixon resigned under the threat of impeachment, and in 1973–74 Watergate was on Canada's front pages, yet he had not subverted his country's Constitution, he had not required Americans to seek proficiency in a minority regional language if they aspired to work for their federal government, nor had he, an admitted practitioner of deceit, used deception to change the American system of government.

Pierre Trudeau resigned not under any risk of impeachment but under the risk of electoral defeat. He had run things for sixteen years; what was the point of risking a recurrence of the "deep pall" that an aide ascribed to him after his near-defeat in 1972?[13]

The condition of the country at the time of his departure — divided, fractious, litigious, and debt-ridden — and for which the policies and political acts he imposed must bear most of the responsibility, would have made a strong case for impeachment. That it was not attempted is no reason for failing to consider whether or not it would have been justified. Rather would it be both just and appropriate to demonstrate the harm that a single-minded man can do to a nominally democratic and federally constituted country through the exercise of legitimate power.

How that power is to be curbed poses a challenge to political scientists as well as to politicians, but if we have learned anything from the Trudeau experience it is surely a need to avoid the rigidities he imposed on us and to restore not only the flexibility that inspires the BNA Act but also the peculiarly Canadian qualities that flowed from it.

Those qualities include a willingness to compromise, not in the sense of surrendering to threats, as Pearson did with the unions and with the challenge from Quebec, nor in the Mulroneyesque sense, copied from union-dominated "collective bargaining," of locking people up until their stamina is as exhausted as their arguments, but in the sense of reaching an accommodation where both sides have made some adjustment to their positions over time.

Over time. Not under the compulsion of one man's yearning for fame in his lifetime, but recognizing that other lifetimes are following their various courses and that the same good sense that inspires juries to approach the truth will animate Canadians in their approaches to self-government.

Now it may be that the convulsions of the Pearson/Trudeau years, and the rough waters that lie ahead for our confederation since the election of an avowedly separatist party to Parliament and the election of a separatist government in Quebec, will conspire to make my dream of restoring the BNA Act to pre-eminence unattainable. Accordingly it is worth spending a few more moments in considering what might be done instead.

SEVEN

We are not alone. Russians and East Europeans are facing challenges far more formidable than ours, Swedes and New Zealanders challenges that are similar, and in which the latter have made remarkable progress. The Chinese are emerging from Mao Tse-tung's disastrous attempt to force an industrious and entrepreneurial people into the straitjacket of communism.

Yet memories are short. "Democratic socialism" may have a nice ring to it, but at the root of it still is the impulse to centralize political power. Pierre Trudeau's susceptibility to that impulse conflicted with his often expressed concern to limit the exercise of all governmental power, yet his Charter of Rights and Freedoms, which was designed to that end, expanded the power of government and proliferated it in agencies, commissions, committees, and tribunals that might be nominally answerable to elected governments but in practice are answerable to themselves.

The point I tried to make in chapter 2 is worth repeating here. When we look at the political spectrum, we see the centre straddled by the moderate views of people who are comfortable with liberal or conservative concepts that are neither too liberal nor too conservative, a democratic compromise that ebbs and flows under the aegis of individual freedom and parliamentary government. It is when the concepts move away from the straddled centre that the trouble starts. It heralds a move toward an extreme that, whether to the left or right, will arrive at the rear of the political circle, diametrically opposed to the democratic compromise it abandoned. But because of the media's predilection for the political Left, we see an unchanging pattern: blind eyes to crimes of the Left; laser searches for crimes of what is identified as the Right.

Friedrich Hayek's warning from across the years is as true today as it was when he wrote it in 1944: "While to many who have watched the transition [in Italy and Germany] from socialism to fascism at close quarters the connection between the two has become increasingly obvious, in the democracies the majority of people still believe that socialism and freedom can be combined. ...That democratic socialism, the great Utopia of the last few generations, is not only unachievable, but that to strive for it produces something so utterly different that few of those who now wish it would be prepared to accept the consequences, many will not believe until the connection has been laid bare in all its aspects."[1]

As recently as November, 1994, when he accepted an honorary doctorate from the University of Toronto, the celebrated Oxford philosopher Isaiah Berlin said, "The first purpose of socialism, apart from social justice, is to give food to the hungry and to clothe the naked. No socialist government has yet succeeded in doing that....One cannot have everything one wants – not only in practice, but even in theory. The denial of this, the search for a single, overarching ideal because it is the one and only true one for humanity, invariably leads to coercion."[2]

In another classic, *How Democracies Perish* (1983), Jean-François Revel wrote: "In 1956, people in the democracies were forced by the Khrushchev report to face the truth about the Stalinist terror....By that time, however, all this held no more than historical interest for the West. The disclosures had come too late to purge Western thinking and politics of the golden legend of communism swallowed between the two world wars. The imposture maintained by Soviet propaganda during those years has had a lasting influence on Western countries' internal politics by diverting the left into a feckless fight for, or at least good will toward, totalitarian socialism."[3]

I couldn't escape the connection between *The Valour and the Horror* and the major role of the CBC in promoting the growth of the state in Canada. The McKenna brothers, and the CBC/NFB insiders who agreed with them, were refugees from the Peace Movement of the 1970s and 1980s that Revel described as exploiting "such wholly justified and respectable, even indispensable, feelings as fear of nuclear war, opposition to war of any kind, the desire for reduction of armaments and of the risk of conflict. It mobilizes Communist parties and labour unions, of course, but it also enlists a large segment of the Socialist International, the British Labour Party, various religious sects in all countries, and the ecologists, as well as great numbers of the unorganized."[4]

In *Maclean's*, September 26, 1994, University of Toronto Professor John Crispo wrote that the McKenna film "so inaccurately denigrated Canada's magnificent contribution to the Allied cause during the Second World War that it represented one of the worst propaganda pieces ever aired here or anywhere else under the guise of a so-called documentary." He noted that when he was "left of centre and a regular fixture on the CBC from the late 1960s until the early 1980s, I did not think much about its left-wing perspective, presumably because I felt very comfortable with it or simply was not conscious of this institutional bias." With the years, he moved to the right of centre "and gradually faded from its radio waves and TV screens." In a snapshot of the self-designated role of Canada's New Class he wrote, "As Knowlton Nash, one of the deans of the CBC's untouchables, said recently on air: 'The role of the journalist is to establish the national agenda.'"

The previous year, Mark Starowicz, a leading figure of the CBC, gave his personal views about public television at the Canadian Embassy in Washington. He said that "Domestic space is being segmented. And transnational space is emerging, but in private hands, and outside the control of the nation state...the so called 'disappearance of public space' will probably have its most profound effect *in the U.S.*, where cost of fragmentation of the body politic will probably exact its greatest price....The impending segmentation of public space...will, I think, create a moral imperative for the United States to assure that free basic television, television that serves the public agenda, is preserved and enlarged. ...For smaller markets, such as Canada...the 1,000 channel universe, once the satellite cracks the regulatory borders, will become a fierce challenge to the nation state's capacity to define its agenda. ...In the television revolution, a nation will either be an aggressive player, or a cultural victim."[5]

When the Berlin Wall was torn down, and Russia ventured upon another revolution, there was rejoicing in the West. When the dead hand of communism was lifted from Eastern Europe, the prospect of political and economic freedom for its oppressed peoples was hailed by liberals as well as conservatives. Conservatives congratulated one another that socialism's inherent fallacies had brought it down before the eyes of the world. Socialism was dead. But liberals, too, as always paying lip service to freedoms they claimed to champion, were quick to distance themselves from the socialism that had so obviously failed, while embracing with renewed fervour the variety that liberals and pseudo-conservatives alike had practiced for a century. The goal of an Omnipotent Universal State was as plain as ever. The collapse of national prototypes merely confirmed the need for omnipotence. Only the tactics must change.

In Canada, the generals of liberalism abandoned the frontal assault of nationalization that had got a bad name, and reinforced the scouting parties that were thought to have good ones. Among the committees for legislating this kind of right and the commissions for extinguishing that kind of wrong, among the groups advocating that this be done or that prevented, could be discerned a common factor: all drew inspiration and funding from the state.

This was the result of the "reforms" to the Constitution which, as Trudeau wrote in his *Memoirs*, "largely enshrined the values I had been advocating since I wrote my first article in *Cité libre* in 1950." Canada had been changed to suit one man's view of the world and it is perhaps fitting to remind ourselves how his view differs from others.

Canada since its inception has been home to two conflicting styles of government, commonly known as the English style, and the French style. In the English style, everyone is free to do anything that is not prohibited by the law of the land – the common law. In the French style, there is no inherent freedom. Rather, the government confers certain rights upon the people through a written charter.

For many years, the English style predominated. It was the outcome of the wish expressed by the leaders of Canada's founding provinces "to be federally united into One Dominion under the Crown of the United Kingdom of Great Britain and Ireland, with a Constitution similar in Principle to that of the United Kingdom." That wish, enacted into law as The British North America Act, 1867, divided Canada into "Four Provinces, named

Ontario, Quebec, Nova Scotia, and New Brunswick."

To accommodate the French-speaking citizens of Quebec, Section 133 stated that "Either the English or the French Language may be used by any Person in the Debates of the Houses of the Parliament of Canada and of the Houses of the Legislature of Quebec," both languages were to be used in "the respective Records and Journals of those Houses," and either could be used in the Federal Court of Canada and the Supreme Court, and any courts of Quebec.

However, for the French-speaking citizens of Quebec, the idea of being part of one dominion that adhered to a form of government and law quite different from the one they had been used to since the days of New France (and which, uniquely in the British Empire, had been reserved to them by the Quebec Act of 1774) – that idea was literally foreign to them. The idea remains foreign to this day, and it was therefore only natural that the politicians and their advisers who initiated major changes to the Act in 1980–2, and who had been schooled in the French tradition, should have rewritten it in the French mode.

Unfortunately, that radical change, while it was thought to be acceptable to the one-quarter of Canadians in Quebec, merely reversed the situation that prevailed before: the form of government that had been foreign to the French-speaking minority had been superseded by a different form that was foreign to the English-speaking majority.

This fundamental contradiction is rooted in the historical context of Confederation. Despite the BNA Act's commitment to a constitution "similar in Principle to that of the United Kingdom," the Act's Canadian framers were also witnesses to the Civil War south of the border. There, they saw two possible circumstances that could threaten the stability of the new dominion. One might arise from a threat of secession; the other from failure to suppress it. The way to prevent those circumstances from arising was to vest the national government with the power "to make Laws for the Peace, Order, and good Government of Canada" in relation to all matters not assigned exclusively to the provinces. As we noted in chapter 1: "...undoubtedly the powers bestowed on the Dominion Government and Parliament are greater when compared with the powers reserved to the Provinces than are the powers which the Constitution of the United States gives to the federal government." However, citing the dominion government's authority to disallow provincial acts as being intended to "prevent any troublesome or dangerous conflict of authority arising between the central and local governments" and thus to avoid recourse to the Courts, Dicey concluded that, "In Canada, as in the United States, the Courts inevitably become the interpreters of the Constitution."

The distinction was underlined both by Lester Pearson's remark about a prime minister's near-dictatorial powers and by Colin Campbell's that "not even the power of appointment of American presidents affords the type of latitude provided by Trudeau's long years in office."

"The Federal system," Lord Acton wrote in his *History of Freedom*, "limits and restrains sovereign power by dividing it, and by assigning to Government only certain defined rights."[6] But in Canada, the federal government is not only assigned certain defined rights, it is enabled, by the exercise of two of those rights, to invade provincial powers as well.

Those two rights, numbers 3 and 4 of section 91, are: "The raising of Money by any Mode or System of Taxation"; and "The borrowing of Money on the Public Credit." Both of them were used from the start to maintain the federal government's fiscal supremacy. Although the provinces had the exclusive right to raise money through direct taxation, the common belief was that such taxation was "uneconomic and subject to large-scale tax evasion, that it would inhibit individual and corporate initiative and, very likely, discourage immigration" (*Canada Year Book*, 1867–1967). Consequently none of them chose that means, and the federal government had to choose between two alternative ways of providing revenue: one was to transfer to the provinces the right to levy certain indirect taxes; the other was to install a system of federal subsidies. The Fathers of Confederation chose the latter, and federal subsidies became an important source of provincial revenue.

Nevertheless, so long as the subsidies were kept within bounds, the system worked. Despite the explosion of government spending during the two world wars, prudent fiscal policies kept the public debt under control and, except for the actual war periods, budgets were in balance until 1959.

It was then that the federal debt began to rise. By 1969, the last year of a budget surplus, the federal debt was $16.222 billion, or 19.8 percent of the Gross National Product.[7]

In February 1991, the Department of Finance wrote in its paper, *The Deficit and the Public Debt*:

By 1984–85, the debt was $206 billion and growing at an annual rate of almost 25 percent. The deficit had reached more than $38 billion. It had two parts:
- $22 billion in interest on the debt; plus
- $16 billion more in spending on programmes and services than was collected in revenues. This was known as the operating deficit.

At that time, the government was handing out $1.33 worth of services for every dollar Canadians paid in federal taxes. It might have looked like a bargain, but it wasn't. We are now paying the price of too much borrowing in the past.[8]

By 1989, the federal debt was over half the GNP. All provinces and municipalities were spending far in excess of the revenues generated by their own taxes, and the total debt of all three levels of government, which had been $58 billion in 1968, was $532 billion, about 85 percent of GNP. As I write, six years later, the combined debt is about $780 billion, roughly equal to the country's economic output.

This dramatic rise in public debt accompanied Canada's political redirection toward a welfare state, in short toward socialism, at a time when socialist experiments worldwide were cracking under debt burdens their failing economies could not sustain. That redirection, as we have seen, was also facilitated by an ingenious manipulation of the flawed federalism that attended the nation's birth. As Felix Morley wrote in his book, *Freedom and Federalism*: "Socialism and federalism are necessarily political opposites, because the former demands that centralized concentration of power which the latter by definition denies.... The essence of

federalism is reservation of control over local affairs to the localities themselves...."[9]

For a century, sufficient fiscal prudence prevailed at all three
levels of government to restrain excesses: the flaws in the federal structure were not critical. They became critical when the federal government set out to centralize authority through a vastly
expanded use of its power to borrow money on the public credit. From the mid-1960s, when provinces were seduced into
"shared-cost" programmes, the Canadian Government's role was
changed. No longer was it bent on securing Peace, Order, and
good Government; it was now the Grand Redistributor, passing
60 percent of its non-interest spending to other governments,
businesses, and individuals. It was in fact borrowing money to pay
the interest on money it had borrowed before; a condition that
put Canada under watch by the International Monetary Fund.

Canada's history is marked by constitutional conferences and
there is nothing unusual about seeking changes to reflect the
changing world – provided they are arrived at with the consent
of the people. In the English tradition that is the function of
Parliament: it passes laws that reflect the changing times and the
laws pass into the common law of which the Constitution consists.

Thus in confronting the need for change to the Canadian Constitution, adherents of the English style might favour recognizing,
without attempting to define, the citizens' inherent, pre-existent,
freedom under the law. They might also favour restricting the
powers of government so that it could never infringe on that
freedom except in a national emergency and then only with the
people's expressed consent.

Adherents of the French style might favour defining the citizens' rights in a manner that would be guaranteed by the state,
and in which public servants would be protected from the consequences of acts performed in the course of their duties. In other
words, an attempt to agree on the style of a national government
would confront the same issue that divides the country today.

From this statement of fact now falls the deduction that the
prime obstacle to Canadian harmony is the Constitution itself.
By dodging the root issue – that in a federal state local affairs
should be handled locally – and by trying to force harmony upon

disparate communities, successive federal governments have denied Canadians the benefits of a true federalism. Consequently, the national constitution could be quite a simple document, confining its provisions to those responsibilities that are national in scope, and leaving everything else to be covered by provincial constitutions that provinces would decide upon in their several ways.

Procrustean attempts by Canadian politicians and their advisers to make the Constitution fit two different beds are bound to fail. Citizens cannot rest in uncomfortable beds; beds moreover they had no hand in choosing.

While Canada's French-speaking citizens form the country's most prominent minority, they are not alone in their distinctness: every citizen is distinct.

In a world grown conscious of a tribe's enduring links, trying to force tribes to fuse within artificial nation states is a proven failure. People want to run their own affairs as much as possible, and a federal state allows them to do that.

In the closing years of the twentieth century, Canadians have the chance to set the troubled world an example that could lead it toward a much less troubled future.

To meet that requirement, my own modest proposal invokes the idea of a constitutional convention or constituent assembly. Not a first ministers' conference; not a select joint committee; not, in short, one more gathering of professional politicians to be harangued by every government-subsidized advocacy group, all claiming to speak with one voice for the multitudes they pester through their mailing lists; not any of these.

Instead I would invite the computer specialists, in conjunction with Elections Canada, to apply to the Canada-wide lists of eligible voters the same method by which juries are selected, and to select a jury.

There is much to be said for juries. That they are democratic is incontestable, for they are composed of people whose prime qualification is that they be members of the *demos*. Whatever standing they may have in society is left at the door of the room they inhabit. Their purpose is to exercise their faculties in the cause of justice.

In the closing paragraphs of his essay *The Twelve Men*, Gilbert Chesterton wrote:

Now, it is a terrible business to mark a man out for the vengeance of men. But it is a thing to which a man can grow accustomed, as he can to other terrible things; he can even grow accustomed to the sun. And the horrible thing about all legal officials, even the best, about all judges, magistrates, barristers, detectives, and policemen, is not that they are wicked (some of them are good), not that they are stupid (several of them are quite intelligent), it is simply that they have got used to it.

Strictly they do not see the prisoner in the dock; all they see is the usual man in the usual place. They do not see the awful court of judgement; they only see their own workshop. Therefore, the instinct of Christian civilization has most wisely declared that into their judgements there shall upon every occasion be infused fresh blood and fresh thoughts from the streets. Men shall come in who can see the court and the crowd, and coarse faces of the policemen and the professional criminals, the wasted faces of the wastrels, the unreal faces of the gesticulating counsel, and see it all as one sees a new picture or play hitherto unvisited.

Our civilization has decided, and very justly decided, that determining the guilt or innocence of men is a thing too important to be trusted to trained men. It wishes for light upon that awful matter, it asks men who know no more law than I know, but who can feel the things that I felt in the jury box. When it wants a library catalogued, or the solar system discovered, or any trifle of that kind, it uses up its specialists. But when it wishes anything done which is really serious it collects twelve of the ordinary men standing around. The same thing was done, if I remember right, by the Founder of Christianity.[10]

The reader may say that this is all very well, but who is to brief your jury beforehand? What task are they to be given and what resources could they call upon? Who is to draw up a bibliography from which they can educate themselves about constitutions?

These questions bring us to the root of the matter. As Lenin said, "Who whom?" Who briefs the briefers? Who describes the task? Who guards the guardians?

The task would be to write a constitution for Canada, and I would suggest one pre-condition: that the names of the twelve be withheld from the press, from the public, and from each other throughout the twelve months that would be set aside for the jury members to educate themselves in the constitutional and political records of the industrialized nations. That is, they would conduct, individually, and using the resources that are readily available to everyone through the library system, a one-year study of how the different countries managed their affairs. At the end of the year they would meet and set about the task.

They would have to be paid from the public purse. If they were employed, the employer would be asked to grant leave of absence for up to two years, and would be sworn to secrecy. If they were housewives and mothers, quite apart from their pay, help would be provided at the public expense. All of them would be sworn to secrecy, permitted only to divulge that they had been picked for a "work of national importance."

Is this fanciful? Could it be kept quiet for two years? Why not? We kept a lot of things quiet pretty successfully for the six years 1939–45. The same thing is done with Cabinet papers and whatever happens in the Privy Council Office.

Let us suppose that it worked, that following their twelve-month sabbatical our twelve jury members met at the appointed time and place, that they elected a man or woman as foreman and got down to business.

Inevitably, each one would bring to the table some preconception of what should be done. But in the course of their deliberations a process would be at work. Twelve Canadians would be exhibiting the characteristics that I believe to be endemic: polite, but blunt when necessary; practical and down to earth; independent yet ready to help (but not to interfere); not class conscious.

Perhaps it is fanciful. Readers will think of many objections, but even to consider the possibility reminds us how such a process differs from Pierre Trudeau's revolutionary method, and from Brian Mulroney's subsequent assaults by way of Meech Lake and

Charlottetown. There, the assembled ministers and their personal staffs, and the professional advisers of the federal and provincial civil services, strove to get as much of their preconceived ideas not only on to the agenda but into the final drafts. Battling them all the time were the chattering classes in print, on air and screen, repeating their own preconceived ideas to bewildered audiences, while outside the conference rooms that other class — the mostly State-subsidized advocates for or opponents of a myriad private causes — jumped up and down before the cameras.

Does our postulated jury sound so bad compared to those circuses? How many readers tried to get their personal opinions into the conference rooms? How many who did so were vouchsafed any acknowledgement of the effort? How many had confidence in the first ministers who hadn't asked them for opinions but were going ahead anyway?

I suggest that we want to avoid a repetition of the circuses. We have learned not to trust the trained men in their accustomed places, but we have to trust someone.

There is much to be said for volunteers, for people who feel strongly enough about a cause to give their own time to it. Suppose we were to mix three ingredients: jury principle (members of the *demos*); election (gaining confidence of the *demos*); and federalism (local affairs governed locally; national affairs nationally)?

Such a mixture might evolve in three stages: first, publication of An Intention to Write a Constitution for Canada, CONSTITUTION 2000; second, recruitment of volunteers; and third, election of a Constitutional Representative from each province and territory, twelve in all.

Funding for the initial publication? By subscription of individual citizens. No corporate sponsors, no appeals to governments.

Volunteers? Will volunteer.

Candidates for election? Canadian citizens or landed immigrants, but no present or former members of federal, provincial, or municipal governments.

Yes, it would have to be structured. Yes, it would need leaders to get it off the ground. Yes, there would be problems of every kind.

But wouldn't it be worth a shot?

At the beginning I wrote that Canada is above all a place where people tolerate their neighbours and settle differences by peaceful means. The differences that are neither trivial nor transitory will not go away: for them, settlement implies acceptance of the differences in the way that neighbours tolerate their neighbours. A national government that confined its activities to national matters, such as foreign affairs, sound money, and national defence, would have no impact on those local differences: it would have no role and it would not be involved.

The differences that remained would be local matters, to be resolved or tolerated locally.

Once the idea of a CONSTITUTION 2000 gets around, I suspect that the people the country needs will get around to it. They, who will bring the qualities I've mentioned to the aid of this great country, will respond to the call.

• APPENDIX •

THE BRITISH NORTH
AMERICA ACTS 1867 TO 1975

VI. – Distribution of Legislative Powers

Powers of the Parliament

91. It shall be lawful for the Queen, by and with the Advice and Consent of the Senate and House of Commons, to make Laws for the Peace, Order, and good Government of Canada, in relation to all Matters not coming within the Classes of Subjects by this Act assigned exclusively to the Legislatures of the Provinces; and for greater Certainty, but not so as to restrict the Generality of the foregoing Terms of this Section, it is hereby declared that (notwithstanding anything in this Act) the exclusive Legislative Authority of the Parliament of Canada extends to all Matters coming within the Classes of Subjects next herein-after enumerated; that is to say, –

1. The amendment from time to time of the Constitution of Canada, except as regards matters coming within the classes of subjects by this Act assigned exclusively to the Legislatures of the provinces, or as regards rights or privileges by this or any other Constitutional Act granted or secured to the Legislature or the Government of a province, or to any class of persons with respect to schools or as regards the use of the English or the French language or as regards the requirements that there shall be a session of the Parliament of Canada at least once each year, and that no House of Commons shall continue for more than five years from the day of the return of the Writs for choosing the House: provided, however, that a House of Commons may in time of real or apprehended war, invasion or insurrection be continued

by the Parliament of Canada if such continuation is not opposed by the votes of more than one-third of the members of such House. [1949; repealed 1982]

1A. The Public Debt and Property.
 2. The Regulation of Trade and Commerce.
2A. Unemployment insurance. [1940]
 3. The raising of Money by any Mode or System of Taxation.
 4. The borrowing of Money on the Public Credit.
 5. Postal Service.
 6. The Census and Statistics.
 7. Militia, Military and Naval Service, and Defence.
 8. The fixing of and providing for the Salaries and Allowances of Civil and other Officers of the Government of Canada.
 9. Beacons, Buoys, Lighthouses, and Sable Island.
10. Navigation and Shipping.
11. Quarantine and the Establishment and Maintenance of Marine Hospitals.
12. Sea Coast and Inland Fisheries.
13. Ferries between a Province and any British or Foreign Country or between Two Provinces.
14. Currency and Coinage.
15. Banking, Incorporation of Banks, and the Issue of Paper Money.
16. Savings Banks.
17. Weights and Measures.
18. Bills of Exchange and Promissory Notes.
19. Interest.
20. Legal Tender.
21. Bankruptcy and Insolvency.
22. Patents of Invention and Discovery.
23. Copyrights.
24. Indians, and Lands reserved for the Indians.
25. Naturalization and Aliens.
26. Marriage and Divorce.
27. The Criminal Law, except the Constitution of

Courts of Criminal Jurisdiction, but including the Procedure in Criminal Matters.

28. The Establishment, Maintenance, and Management of Penitentiaries.

29. Such Classes of Subjects as are expressly excepted in the Enumeration of the Classes of Subjects by this Act assigned exclusively to the Legislatures of the Provinces.

And any Matter coming within any of the Classes of Subjects enumerated in this Section shall not be deemed to come within the Class of Matters of a local or private Nature comprised in the Enumeration of the Classes of Subjects by this Act assigned exclusively to the Legislatures of the Provinces.

Exclusive Powers of Provincial Legislatures

92. In each Province the Legislature may exclusively make Laws in relation to Matters coming within the Classes of Subjects next herein-after enumerated; that is to say,—

1. The Amendment from Time to Time, notwith-standing anything in this Act, of the Constitution of the Province, except as regards the Office of Lieutenant Governor. [repealed 1982]

2. Direct Taxation within the Province in order to the raising of a Revenue for Provincial Purposes.

3. The borrowing of Money on the sole Credit of the Province.

4. The Establishment and Tenure of Provincial Offices and the Appointment and Payment of Provincial Officers.

5. The Management and Sale of the Public Lands belonging to the Province and of the Timber and Wood thereon.

6. The Establishment, Maintenance, and Management of Public and Reformatory Prisons in and for the Province.

7. The Establishment, Maintenance, and Management of Hospitals, Asylums, Charities, and Eleemosynary Institutions in and for the Province, other than Marine Hospitals.

8. Municipal Institutions in the Province.

9. Shop, Saloon, Tavern, Auctioneer, and other Licences in order to the raising of a Revenue for Provincial, Local, or Municipal Purposes.

10. Local Works and Undertakings other than such as are of the following Classes:—

    (a) Lines of Steam or other Ships, Railways, Canals, Telegraphs, and other Works and Undertakings connecting the Province with any other or others of the Provinces, or extending beyond the Limits of the Province;

    (b) Lines of Steam Ships between the Province and any British or Foreign Country;

    (c) Such Works as, although wholly situate within the Province, are before or after their Execution declared by the Parliament of Canada to be for the general Advantage of Canada or for the Advantage of Two or more of the Provinces.

11. The Incorporation of Companies with Provincial Objects.

12. The Solemnization of Marriage in the Province.

13. Property and Civil Rights in the Province.

14. The Administration of Justice in the Province, including the Constitution, Maintenance, and Organization of Provincial Courts, both of Civil and of Criminal Jurisdiction, and including Procedure in Civil Matters in those Courts.

15. The Imposition of Punishment by Fine, Penalty, or Imprisonment for enforcing any Law of the Province made in relation to any Matter coming within any of the Classes of Subjects enumerated in this Section.

16. Generally all Matters of a merely local or private Nature in the Province.

Education

93. In and for each Province the Legislature may exclusively make Laws in relation to Education, subject and according to the following Provisions: —

(1) Nothing in any such Law shall prejudicially affect any Right or Privilege with respect to Denominational Schools which any Class of Persons have by Law in the Province at the Union:

(2) All the Powers, Privileges, and Duties at the Union by Law conferred and imposed in Upper Canada on the Separate Schools and School Trustees of the Queen's Roman Catholic Subjects shall be and the same are hereby extended to the Dissentient Schools of the Queen's Protestant and Roman Catholic Subjects in Quebec:

(3) Where in any Province a System of Separate or Dissentient Schools exists by Law at the Union or is thereafter established by the Legislature of the Province, an Appeal shall lie to the Governor General in Council from any Act or Decision of any Provincial Authority affecting any Right of Privilege of the Protestant or Roman Catholic Minority of the Queen's Subjects in relation to Education:

(4) In case any such Provincial Law as from Time to Time seems to the Governor General in Council requisite for the due Execution of the Provisions of this Section is not made, or in case any Decision of the Governor General in Council on any Appeal under this Section is not duly executed by the proper Provincial Authority in that Behalf, then and in every such Case, and as far only as the Circumstances of each Case require, the Parliament of Canada may make remedial Laws for the due Execution of the Provisions of this Section and of any Decision of the Governor General in Council under this Section.

IX. – Miscellaneous Provisions

[The first five paragraphs of this Section cover, respectively, Oath of Allegiance, etc.; Continuance of existing Laws, Courts, Officers, etc.; Transfer of Officers to Canada; Appointment of new Officers; and Treaty Obligations. The last is **133.**]

133. Either the English or French Language may be used by any Person in the Debates of the Houses of the Parliament of Canada and of the Houses of the Legislature of Quebec; and both those Languages shall be used in the respective Records and Journals of those Houses; and either of those Languages may be used by any Person or in any Pleading or Process in or issuing from any Court of Canada established under this Act, and in or from all or any of the Courts of Quebec.

The Acts of the Parliament of Canada and of the Legislature of Quebec shall be printed and published in both those Languages.

• NOTES •

1. The Royal Commission on Bilingualism and Biculturalism, 1967–70.
2. *Toronto Sun*, March 22, 1992.
3. *federalism and political community: Essays in Honour of Donald Smiley* (Peterborough: broadview press, 1989), pp. 113, 134.
4. *The Globe and Mail*, April 21, 1992.
5. *Vancouver Province*, December 4, 1981.
6. Colin Campbell, *Governments under stress* (Toronto: University of Toronto Press, 1983), p. 93.
7. Alain Peyrefitte, *The Trouble with France* (New York: Alfred A. Knopf, 1981), p. 209.
8. *Canada Year Book*, 1867–1967, p. 28.
9. A.V. Dicey, *The Law of the Constitution* (Indianapolis: Liberty Fund, 1982), pp. 94–5.
10. David Somerville, *Trudeau Revealed* (Toronto: BMG Publishing, 1978), p. 195.
11. Pierre Elliott Trudeau, *Memoirs* (Toronto: McClelland & Stewart, 1993), p. 328.
12. Campbell, *Governments*, p. 96.
13. Ibid., p. 96.
14. Stuart Chase, *The Tyranny of Words* (New York: Harcourt, Brace & World, 1938), p. 100.
15. Felix Morley, *Freedom and Federalism* (Chicago: Henry Regnery Company, 1959), p. 5.
16. In her book *Implosion* (Montreal: Institute for Research on Public Policy, 1986), Nicole Morgan wrote that between 1965 and 1975 the federal public service doubled. In *Legion* magazine, August 1984, in his article "Yes, Minister," journalist Dave McIntosh wrote that "It expanded in the late 1960s and 1970s at a rate of 10–12 per cent a year. Works

Minister Jean-Eudes Dubé put it all in a nutshell when he said to the construction industry: 'Put up the office buildings. We'll fill 'em up.'"

17. *The Globe and Mail*, August 6, 1994.

18. J.A. Laponce, *Languages and Their Territories* (Toronto: University of Toronto Press, 1987), p. 33. Quoted in *federalism*, p. 169.

19. *Toronto Sun*, April 8, 1990.

20. John Stuart Mill, *On Liberty* (Northbrook: AHM Publishing Corporation, 1947), p. 55.

21. Average of weekly bank rate settings, January 1985 to June 1991, per Bank of Canada textcomm to author, June 14, 1991.

Chapter 2

1. William Gairdner, *The Trouble With Canada* (Toronto: Stoddart, 1990), pp. 132–3.

2. *Freemen Digest* (Provo: The Center for Global Studies, 1979), pp. 1, 6.

3. John R. Ferguson, in a private paper, *Pathway to Prosperity: The free-market solution to increasing Canada's productivity*, December 1994, argues powerfully in favour of a return to free-market principles, shows how a single rate of tax at 15% applied to the three classes of income (corporate, personal, and investment above an agreed minimum to protect the needy), would have delivered a surplus in the federal government's 1992 accounts towards debt repayment; and this *with no other taxes, direct or indirect*. Also, for the first time to my knowledge, he has determined a way to measure productivity in both private and public sectors.

As for eliminating the debt, an imaginative proposal, *Phoenix Rising*, published by Toronto's Strategic Analysis Corporation in 1995, offers a practical means of restoring fiscal probity to all Canadian governments. By applying to government's debt burden the same principle that corporations apply in their periodic restructurings (that is, converting debt to equity), Ross Healy and Enrico Sgromo have devised a practical and, to investors, attractive, instrument that would deliver Canadians from their debt burden and effectively realize the prosperous future that fiscal mismanagement has so long delayed.

4. Jack Pickersgill, quoted in Christina McCall-Newman, *Grits* (Toronto: Macmillan of Canada, 1982), p. 45.

5. Dr. Warren J. Blackman, Professor of Monetary Theory, University of Calgary, quoted in Verne Atrill, *The Freedom Manifesto* (Calgary: Dimensionless Science Publications, 1981), p. i.

6. Tom Kent, *A Public Purpose* (Montreal: McGill-Queen's University Press, 1988), p. 366.

7. Bertrand de Jouvenel, *The Ethics of Redistribution* (Indianapolis: Liberty Press, 1952), p. 72.

8. Friedrich A. Hayek, *The Road to Serfdom,* 2nd edition (Chicago: University of Chicago Press, 1976), pp. xi–xii.

9. *Consensus* (The National Citizens' Coalition), August 1985, p.4.

10. *Content*, September/October, 1990.

11. *Canadian Economic Observer, May 1993*, Bank of Canada Review, Winter – 1993–94.

12. George Bain, *GOTCHA! How the Media Distort the News* (Toronto: Key Porter, 1994), pp. 51–2.

13. Stevie Cameron, *On The Take: Crime, Corruption and Greed in the Mulroney Years* (Toronto: MacFarlane, Walter and Ross, 1994).

14. Hayek, *Road*, p. 30, n. 9.

15. *The Globe and Mail*'s *Report on Business* magazine (June 1993): 49.

Chapter 3

1. *The Globe and Mail*, September 13, 1994.

2. *Toronto Sun*, February 19, 1979.

3. Morley, *Freedom*, pp. 3–4.

4. Pierre Elliott Trudeau, *Federalism and the French Canadians* (Toronto: Macmillan of Canada, 1968), p. 125.

5. Ibid., p. 127.

6. Ibid., p. 27.

7. *Encyclopedia Britannica*, 1946, vol. 20, p. 890.

8. Trudeau, *Federalism*, p. 124.
9. Richard Gwyn, *The Northern Magus* (Toronto: McClelland & Stewart, 1980), pp. 69–70.
10. Trudeau, *Federalism*, p. 128.
11. Trudeau, *Memoirs*, p. 309.
12. Christina McCall-Newman, *Grits*, p. 303.
13. Trudeau, *Memoirs*, p. 252.
14. Campbell, *Governments*, p. 99.
15. *federalism*, pp. 428–9.
16. Quoted in the Hon. James Richardson's Brief to the Special Joint Committee of the Senate and of the House of Commons of Canada on the Proposed Resolution for a Joint Address to Her Majesty the Queen respecting the Constitution of Canada on December 16, 1980, p. 8.
17. [British] House of Commons Debates March 3, 1982, 351, 364, 374–7; pp. 187, 193, 198–200.
18. *federalism*, p. 232. Also, Madam Justice Rosalie Abella, of the Ontario appeal court, was quoted in the *Globe*, April 7, 1995, as seeing a strong role for judges in making new law when the occasion demands. "Is there a role for the court as the conscience of the community, giving expression to ideas as a means of educating and directing society's thoughts?" she wrote in a 1981 article. Her answer: "In family law, more than any other area of law, the courts and legislature are 'partners in the enterprise of lawmaking.'"
19. Peyrefitte, *Trouble*, p. 184.

Chapter 4

1. *Consensus* (The National Citizens' Coalition), January 1977, quoting a *Canadian Press* report from London.
2. *Financial Post*, February 3, 1979.
3. *House of Commons, Debates*, July 3, 1981, and *Bank of Canada Review*, May 1988, G1, G4.
4. Provided to the author by Joel Aldred from his notes on a conversation with Bora Laskin on the second floor of the West Block, Parliament Buildings, Ottawa, April 20, 1982.
5. Gordon Robertson, *Canada and the New Constitution* (Montreal:

The Institute for Research on Public Policy, 1983), p. x.
6. Trudeau, *Federalism*, p. 126.
7. Ibid., p. vii.
8. *Starweek*, January 8–15, 1994.
9. Secretary of State for Canada, quoted in *The Taxpayer*, Ontario edition (January/February 1994).
10. *Canada Year Book*, 1992, pp. 88–9.
11. Statistics Canada, *Home Language and Mother Tongue*, catalogue 93–317, Table 1. French total for Ontario was 300,085 from a total population of 9,977,050. Those with French as home language represented 3 percent or less of the population in all provinces and territories except for Quebec (84 percent) and New Brunswick (32 percent). Outside Quebec, and including New Brunswick, only 2.25 percent spoke French at home.
12. Trudeau, *Federalism*, p. 127.
13. Scott Reid, *Lament for a Notion* (Vancouver: Arsenal Pulp Press, 1993), pp. 113, 248-50.

Chapter 5

1. *The Globe and Mail*, September 30, 1982.
2. *federalism*, p. 161.
3. Pierre Elliott Trudeau, *La Nouvelle Trahison des Clercs*, quoted in Somerville, *Trudeau*, p. 157n.
4. *Canada Year Book*, 1973, p. 172.
5. Immigration Minister Sergio Marchi said greater emphasis on European immigration "may mean greater promotion on behalf of immigration for independent skilled or business immigrants because the family class is not being filled by Canadians of European descent." *The Globe and Mail*, September 13, 1994.
6. "Currently, 45.6 percent of immigrants don't know either official language and only about half of these receive federal support for language training because of the high cost." *The Globe and Mail*, October 29, 1994.
7. In a letter published in *UBC Reports*, January 9, 1992, Campbell wrote: "Academic studies at the universities of Western Ontario and Simon Fraser show a steady decline in

productivity of immigrants arriving over the last quarter century. Western Ontario studies differentiate between traditional immigrant groups and new immigrant groups. Those from traditional sources have fallen from 95 percent to 35 percent of all immigrants and maintain a level of productivity (expressed as income) above the Canadian average while those from the new groups have increased from 5 percent to 65 percent of all immigrants and the productivity of the most recent entries has dropped to a level 25 percent below the average of other Canadians."

On October 26, 1994, Jeffrey Simpson wrote in *The Globe and Mail*: "Preliminary data from the Department of Citizenship and Immigration show that compared to average earnings for the general population of $434.60 a week, independent immigrants earn $481.34, entrepreneurial immigrants $502, assisted relatives $420.33 and other family-class immigrants $405. A study from 1980 to 1988 showed a widening gap throughout the period between earnings of independents and family-class immigrants. An Australian study revealed exactly the same trends."

8. "Canada has a large and growing number of working poor. From 1981 to 1986, the under $6/hour employment category grew faster than all other categories combined. This is directly attributable to a high rate of immigration and a failure on the government's part to invest in its own people.

"With the highest rate of immigration in the western world over the past 30 years, Canada had the fastest growing labour force and the lowest investment per new worker. Our rate of productivity is the lowest of any industrialized country and our industrial base, the real engine of wealth production, is disintegrating.

"To be able to say that immigration is a benefit to Canadians, you would have to make the case that Canadians' incomes have increased with higher rates of immigration. All of our large economic models and our economic history have shown that idea to be completely wrong." John Meyer, Zero Population Growth of Canada Inc., in a letter to the *Toronto Star*, September 28, 1991.

9. *Canada Year Book*, 1975, p. 208.

10. Except where noted otherwise, source of immigration figures for the respective years is the department's Annual Report to Parliament on Immigration Levels.

11. In 1986, when 5,088 immigrants were allowed into Canada from Great Britain, 28,000 British emigrants went to Australia. The Australian points system encouraged independent immigrants. Of the required 95 points, 70–75 were awarded to an applicant with a bona fide trade certificate and experience. Knowledge of English brought 15 points, age under 39 brought another 10. Over 80 percent of those who made an initial application to the Australian High Commission in London were approved. By contrast, an applicant with those same qualifications would have been rejected by Canada. The Canadian High Commission in London was getting about 2,000 applications every month, and about 80 percent were rejected outright, that is, before applicants could even fill out the forms. On a private visit to England, former Mississauga Mayor, and vice-president of the Euro-British Immigration Aid Association, Ronald Searle met at Canada House on May 16, 1991 with the Canadian High Commissioner, Donald Macdonald, who reported the circumstances to Ottawa. However, there has been little change. Although the numbers admitted to Canada from Britain rose after 1986 to a high of 9,172 in 1988, they have not reached that level again. According to the Statistical Branch, Immigration Canada, April 14, 1995, the subsequent figures are: 5,737; 8,217; 7,543; 7,138; 7,154; and (1994) 5,855.

12. These goals are detailed in the 1993 Immigration Act, Part I, Canadian Immigration Policy, para 3, *Objectives*:

> 3. It is hereby declared that Canadian immigration policy and the rules and regulations made under this Act shall be designed and administered in such a manner as to promote the domestic and international interests of Canada recognizing the need
>> (a) to support the attainment of such demographic goals as may be established by the Govern-

ment of Canada in respect of the size, rate of growth, structure and geographic distribution of the Canadian population;

(b) to enrich and strengthen the cultural and social fabric of Canada, taking into account the federal and bilingual character of Canada;

(c) to facilitate the reunion in Canada of Canadian citizens and permanent residents with their close relatives from abroad;...

(f) to ensure that any person who seeks admission to Canada on either a permanent or temporary basis is subject to standards of admission that do not discriminate in a manner inconsistent with the Canadian Charter of Rights and Freedoms;...

13. Secretary of State's department in the Public Accounts 1983–84. By 1993 the associations funded by the department filled 102 pages of the public accounts. The chief policy advisory body, the Canadian Ethnocultural Council, Ottawa, received $145,875. *The Globe and Mail*, April 30, 1993.

14. The Municipality of Metropolitan Toronto, *Metropolitan Toronto and The Greater Toronto Area, 1991 Census Atlas — Series B Data*, January 1995.

15. A poll conducted by Toronto-based Forum Canada Research which surveyed 760 adults between March 21–24, 1995, was said to represent overall opinion outside Quebec (not surveyed because the province, not the federal government, controls immigration policy there). It found three out of five Canadians would favour stopping immigration for five years to absorb newcomers already in the country. *Canadian Press* in the *Globe*, May 18, 1995.

Chapter 6

1. Peter J. Stanlis, *Edmund Burke and the Natural Law* (Lafayette: Huntington House, 1986), p. 57.
2. McCall-Newman, *Grits*, p. 213.
3. Frédéric Bastiat, *The Law* (New York: The Foundation for Economic Education, 1977), p. 31.

4. Edmund A. Opitz, in *Freeman*, October 1987.

5. Somerville, *Trudeau*, p. 133.

6. Claire Bickley, "Trudeau's Voyage," *Toronto Sun*, January 9, 1994, p. TV3.

7. The Bomber Harris Trust, *A Battle for Truth* (Toronto: Ramsay Business Systems, 1994), pp. xv–xvi.

8. Desmond Morton, "The master showman plays again" *Starweek*, January 9, 1994, pp. 4, 6.

9. Desmond Seward, *Napoleon and Hitler* (Viking Penguin, 1989), pp. 296–7.

10. Trudeau, *Memoirs*, p. 322.

11. Peyrefitte, *Trouble*, p. 209.

12. Paul Johnson, *A History of the English People* (London: Weidenfeld and Nicolson, 1985), p. 320.

13. Gwyn, *Northern*, p. 138.

Chapter 7

1. Hayek, *Road*, pp. 30–1.

2. *The Globe and Mail*, November 25, 1994.

3. Jean-François Revel, *How Democracies Perish* (Toronto: Fitzhenry & Whiteside, 1983), p. 168.

4. Ibid., p. 145.

5. Mark Starowicz, *The Gutenberg Revolution of Television: Speculations on the Impact of New Technologies* (paper given at the Canadian Embassy, Washington, March 29, 1993), pp. 15–18.

6. Lord Acton, *History of Freedom*, p. 98, quoted in Friedrich A. Hayek, *The Constitution of Liberty* (Chicago: Henry Regnery Company, 1960), p. 184.

7. *House of Commons, Debates*, July 3, 1981 and *Bank of Canada Review*, May 1988, H2.

8. Department of Finance Canada, *The Deficit and the Public Debt*, February 1991, pp.1–2.

9. Morley, *Freedom*, pp. 3–5.

10. G.K. Chesterton, *Selected Essays* (London: Methuen, 1939), pp. 110–11.

• BIBLIOGRAPHY •

Atrill, Verne. *The Freedom Manifesto*. Calgary: Dimensionless Science Publications, 1981.

Bain, George. *GOTCHA! How the Media Distort the News*. Toronto: Key Porter, 1994.

Bastiat, Frédéric. *The Law*. New York: The Foundation for Economic Education, 1977.

Beck, Stanley M. and Ivan Bernier, ed., *Canada and the New Constitution: The Unfinished Agenda*. Montreal: The Institute for Research on Public Policy, 1983.

The Bomber Harris Trust. *A Battle for Truth: Canadian Aircrews sue the CBC over Death by Moonlight: Bomber Command*. Toronto: Ramsay Business Systems, 1994.

Campbell, Colin. *Governments under stress*. Toronto: University of Toronto Press, 1983.

Chase, Stuart. *The Tyranny of Words*. New York: Harcourt, Brace & World, 1938.

Chesterton, G.K. *Selected Essays*. London: Methuen, 1939.

Dicey, A.V. *The Law of the Constitution*. Indianapolis: Liberty Fund, 1982.

federalism and political community: Essays in Honour of Donald Smiley. Peterborough: broadview press, 1989.

Freemen Digest. Provo: The Center for Global Studies, 1979.

Gairdner, William. *The Trouble With Canada*. Toronto: Stoddart, 1990.

Gwyn, Richard. *The Northern Magus*. Toronto: McClelland & Stewart, 1980.

Hayek, Friedrich A. *The Road to Serfdom*. 2nd ed. Chicago: University of Chicago Press, 1976.

Hayek, Friedrich. A. *The Constitution of Liberty*. Chicago: Henry Regnery Company, 1960.

Johnson, Paul. *A History of the English People*. London: Weidenfeld and Nicolson, 1985.

Jouvenel, Bertrand de. *The Ethics of Redistribution*. Indianapolis: Liberty Press, 1952.

Kent, Tom. *A Public Purpose*. Montreal: McGill-Queen's University Press, 1988.

McCall-Newman, Christina. *Grits*. Toronto: Macmillan of Canada, 1982.

Metropolitan Toronto and The Greater Toronto Area, 1991 Census Atlas — Series B Data. Toronto: Municipality of Metropolitan Toronto, 1995.

Mill, John Stuart. *On Liberty*. Northbrook: AHM Publishing Corporation, 1947.

Morgan, Nicole. *Implosion*. Montreal: Institute for Research on Public Policy, 1986.

Morley, Felix. *Freedom and Federalism*. Chicago: Henry Regnery Company, 1959.

Peyrefitte, Alain. *The Trouble with France*. New York: Alfred A. Knopf, 1981.

Reid, Scott. *Lament for a Notion*. Vancouver: Arsenal Pulp Press, 1993.

Revel, Jean-François. *How Democracies Perish*. Toronto: Fitzhenry & Whiteside, 1983.

Seward, Desmond. *Napoleon and Hitler*. Viking Penguin, 1989.

Somerville, David. *Trudeau Revealed*. Toronto: BMG Publishing, 1978.

Stanlis, Peter J. *Edmund Burke and the Natural Law.* Lafayette: Huntington House, 1986.

Trudeau, Pierre Elliott. *Federalism and the French Canadians.* Toronto: Macmillan of Canada, 1968.

Trudeau, Pierre Elliott. *Memoirs.* Toronto: McClelland & Stewart, 1993.

· INDEX ·